*The People of*
# DUNDEE and ANGUS
## at Home and Abroad
## 1800-1850

### By David Dobson

CLEARFIELD

Copyright © 2022
by David Dobson
All Rights Reserved

Published for Clearfield Company by
Genealogical Publishing Company
Baltimore, Maryland
2022

ISBN 9780806359397

## Introduction

This book identifies residents in the adjacent counties of Dundee and Angus, as well as emigrants from there, between 1800 and 1850. Dundee and Angus now form distinct Scottish administrative units but were formerly a single district known as Forfarshire. There were nearly 60 parishes in Forfarshire. The main towns were Brechin, Forfar, and Kirriemuir in Strathmore, with Dundee, Broughty Ferry, Monifieth, Arbroath, and Montrose along the coast.

Angus, which is in the east of Scotland, is divided by a geological fault known as the Highland Line, with the Highlands to the north-west and the Lowlands to the south-east. From the medieval period to the Victorian era Forfar was the administrative centre of Angus or Forfarshire while Dundee, still within Angus, was fast becoming the main industrial and port city. By the late nineteenth century Dundee had become one of the biggest cities in Scotland, famous for its 'jam, jute, and journalism'.

This book contains references to people from Dundee and Angus, at home and abroad, between 1800 and 1850. The information is derived from a wide range of sources such as court records, contemporary newspapers and journals, monumental inscriptions, and documents found in archives. The entries bring together emigrants, their destinations-- especially in North America, the West Indies, and Australasia-- with their kin who remained in Scotland.

The late 18th and early 19th centuries marked a period of rapid changes in this part of Scotland. The Agricultural Revolution and the Industrial Revolution led to the formation of larger farms, forcing the surplus rural population to drift to the rapidly expanding factory towns. For example, in Angus the land-loom weavers, who produced textiles in their homes, were replaced by textile mills in Dundee or Arbroath. The textile industry, which produced linen and canvas, was dependent on imported flax which mainly came from Russia and the Baltic countries, and was supplied to markets in Britain, America, and the West Indies. Jute, brought from India, became the main raw material used in the local textile mills later in the century. For their part, Dundee, Arbroath, and Montrose were fishing and whaling ports and centres of shipbuilding.

A crucial source for this era of Scottish history is the Statistical Report of Scotland (the O.S.A.), established by Sir John Sinclair, The O.S.A. was a collection of reports by nearly one thousand parish ministers in Scotland compiled between 1791 and 1799. These reports cover a wide range of topics for each parish, including geography, education, history, agriculture, shipping, population, and religious denominations. The O.S.A. is therefore a unique source of useful background for the family historian as it provides an insight to Scottish society at the end of the eighteenth century.

The rapid changes in Scottish society in the early 1800s ultimately resulted in the New Statistical Report being researched between 1832 and 1845. Both it and the O.S.A. were published (copies of which many be found in most of the older libraries in Scotland), however they are both available online on the website of the National Library of Scotland. Another recommended book for research into Dundee and Angus families is Alexander Warden's 'Angus or Forfarshire' [five volumes] published in 1880. These volumes should enable researchers with roots in Forfarshire to put their family into a historical context.

David Dobson
Dundee, Scotland, 2021

# REFERENCES

AA   Angus Archives, Restenneth

ABR   Arbroath Burgess Roll

AJ   Aberdeen Journal, series

ANY   St Andrew's Society of New York

AP   St Andrew's Society of Philadelphia

AVR   Angus Valuation Roll

BA   Officers of the Bengal Army

BM   Blackwood's Magazine, series

CG   City Gazette, series

CSG   Campbells & other Glengarry, Stormont & Harrington Pioneers

DBR   Dundee Burgess Roll

DCA   Dundee City Archives

DD   Dundee Directory

DE   Dundee Episcopalians, 1715-1815

DLS   Directory of Landowners in Scotland

DPCA   Dundee, Perth and Cupar Advertiser, series

DSR   Dundee Shipping Register

DYB   Dundee Year Book

EA   Edinburgh Advertiser, series

EC   Edinburgh Courant, series

EEC   Edinburgh Evening Courant, series

EFR   East Fife Record, series

F   Fasti Ecclesiae Scoticanae

FJ  Fife Journal, series

GM  Gentleman's Magazine, series

HS  History Scotland, series

JJ  John o' Groats Journal, series

KCA  King's College, Aberdeen

LCL  Leith Commercial Lists, series

LNA  Lower Norfolk County Antiquary

MCA  Marischal College, Aberdeen

MBR  Montrose Burgess Roll

MG  Montreal Gazette, series

NARA  National Archives, Records Administration

NBC  New Brunswick Courier, series

NRS  National Records of Scotland

PAPEI  Public Archives, Prince Edward Island

QM  Quebec Mercury, series

S  Scotsman, series

SG  Scottish Guardian, series

SLH  Scottish Local History, series

SM  Scots Magazine, series

SPI  Skye Pioneers and the Island

SRA  Strathclyde Regional Archives

TNA  The National Archives

UPC  United Presbyterian Church

W  Witness, series

Glamis Castle, Angus

Broughty Castle, Dundee

Cortachy Castle, Angus

Church of St. Vigeans, Arbroath, Angus

Arbroath, Angus

Round Tower and Cathedral of Brechin, Angus

THE PEOPLE OF DUNDEE & ANGUS, AT HOME & ABROAD 1800-1850

ABBOT, DAVID, master of the Nancy of Dundee in 1795. [NRS.CE70.1.8/7]

ABBOT, JAMES, master of the Alexander of Dundee in 1796, [NRS.CE70.1.8/70]; master of the Amelia of Dundee in 1809, [DD]; residing in Tyndall's Wynd in 1809, and in Castle Court, Dundee, in 1818, [DD]; testament, 1815, Comm. St Andrews. [NRS]

ABBOT, JAMES, master of the London Packet of Dundee trading between St Petersburg, Russia, and Dundee in 1818. [NRS.E504.11.21]

ABBOT, JANET, born 1752, wife of William Wilkie in Lochee, died in 1814. [Howff gravestone, Dundee]

ABBOT, ROBERT, master of the Robert and Jean of Dundee in 1795, [NRS.CE70.1. 58/77]; testament, 1806, Comm. Brechin. [NRS] in 1824. [DSR]

ABBOT, ROBERT, master of the Isobel and Peggy of Dundee in 1809, [DD]; residing in Fish Street, Dundee, in 1809, [DD]; master of the Olive of Dundee in 1824. [DSR]

ABBOT, THOMAS, in Dundee, a salmon fisher at West Ferry, a Precept of Removal, 1815. [NRS.GD45.18.2358]4]

ABERDEIN, JAMES, born 1807 in Dundee, died in Jefferson County, Indiana, in 1881. [S.11,784]

ABERDEEN, JOHN, in Montrose, correspondence, between 1839 and 1850 with his cousin John Lamb in Malda, West Bengal, India. [NRS.GD1.633.5]

ABERDEIN, JOHN, son of John Aberdein a merchant in Montrose, a student at Marischal College, Aberdeen, in 1830s. [MCA]

ABERDEIN, WILLIAM, born 1743, a merchant in Montrose, died in 1810, husband of Christian Stephen, born 1741, died in 1824. [Montrose gravestone]

ADAM, ALEXANDER, master of Alexander of Dundee in 1809. [DD]

ADAM, ALEXANDER, in Douly, Edzell, a Precept of Removal, 1815. [NRS.GD45.18.2358]

ADAM, DAVID, born 1751, a shipmaster in Dundee, died in 1797. [Howff gravestone, Dundee]

ADAM, JAMES, a lease in Linlathen in 1844. [NRS.GD16.28.550]

ADAM, JOHN, born 1792 in Forfar, was educated at Edinburgh University, a surgeon in the Service of the Honourable East India Company in Bengal from 1817 to his death in Calcutta on 29 July 1830. [South Park gravestone, Calcutta, India]

ADAM, JOHN, son of John Adam a surgeon in Forfar, a student at Marischal College in 1808. [MCA]

ADAMS, JOHN, son of Charles Adams a merchant in Forfar, a student at Marischal College, Aberdeen, around 1812. [MCA]

ADAMS, PETER, master of the Spinks of Dundee in 1824. [DSR]

ADAM, WILLIAM, born 15 September 1837- died 15 September 1890, master of the whaling ships Arctic from 1859, and of the Arctic II from 1875 to 1883, also the Maud from 1884 to 1890, father of William Adam, born in 1869, and died in 1942, master of various whaling ships. [HS.18.1.17]; caught 13 whales in the Davis Straits in 1881, and 8235 seals off Newfoundland in 1883. [DYB]

ADAMSON, JAMES, line manager aboard the Princess Charlotte of Dundee bound for the Davis Strait in 1824. [NRS.E508.129.8]

ADAMSON, WILLIAM, born 1778, died 1859, master of several whaling ships from 1808 until 1838. [NRS.E508.115.8]; in Crichton Street, Dundee, in 1818, [DD], master of the Tay of Dundee 1813, trading between St Petersburg, Russia, and Dundee in 1818. [NRS.E508.115.8; 24.21]; master of the Princess Charlotte of Dundee in 1825. [DSR]

ADDISON, JOHN, a merchant in Montrose, testament, 1797, Comm. Brechin. [NRS]

ADDISON, THOMAS, born 1766 in Angus, a schoolmaster who settled in Canada in 1794, died in St John, New Brunswick, on 3 January 1837. [NBC.7.1.1837]

AIKEN, DAVID, from Forfar, a student in Marischal College around 1800. [MCA]

AIKENHEAD, THOMAS, a shipmaster in Arbroath, testament, 1804, Comm. St Andrews. [NRS]

AIMER, JAMES, a joiner from Westhaven, with family, emigrated via Dundee aboard the Providence of Perth, master Robert Nicoll, bound for New York in May 1819. [NRS.CE70.1.15]

AINSLIE, JOHN, a merchant in Rotterdam, Zealand, was admitted as a burgess of Arbroath in 1791. [ABR]

AIR, DAVID, a wright and militiaman, was admitted as a burgess of Arbroath in 1797. [AA.18.941]

AIR, WILLIAM, born 1846, a ships carpenter who was drowned off Peru on 30 October 1869, son of James Air and his wife Catherine Milne. [Friockheim gravestone]

AIRTH, ALEXANDER, versus John Erskine of Dun, re the Mains of Dun, 1806-1809. [NRS.GD123.456]

AIRTH, DAVID, master of the Hannah of Dundee from Leven bound for Montreal on 28 March 1834. [FJ.60]

AIRTH, JOHN, was admitted as a wright burgess of Arbroath in 1797. [AA.18.941]

AITKEN, ALEXANDER, son of Reverend Alexander Aitken in Forfar, a student at Marischal College, Aberdeen, in 1790s. [MCA]

AITKIN, JOHN, born 1726, a schoolmaster of Arbroath in 1748, minister of St Vigeans from 1754 until 1816. [F.5.450]

AITKEN, JOHN, son of Reverend James Aitken in Kirriemuir, graduated MA from Marischal College, Aberdeen, in 1807, later a surgeon in Aberdeen. [MCA]

AITKEN, THOMAS, sailor aboard the Princess Charlotte of Dundee, bound for the Davis Strait in 1824. [NRS.E508.129.8]

AITKENHEAD, THOMAS, born 1767, a shipmaster in Arbroath, died in Riga, Latvia, in 1804, husband of Elizabeth Dall. [Arbroath Abbey gravestone]

ALEXANDER, CATHERINE, born 1825, wife of James Ford, died in Sandhurst, Australia, on 16 August 1858. [Rosehill gravestone, Montrose]

ALEXANDER, DAVID, from Montrose, settled in Petersburg, Virginia, by 1809. [NRS.S/H.1809]

ALEXANDER, JAMES, a preacher and schoolmaster at Ingliston of Eassie, later in Dundee, testament, 1796, Comm. Brechin. [NRS]

ALEXANDER, JAMES, a mason in Montrose, versus Robert Clark a writer in Montrose, in 1827. [NRS.CS228.A9.39]

ALEXANDER, JAMES, and his wife Elizabeth Young in St Vigeans, parents of James Alexander, born 1853, died in Timaru, New Zealand, on 24 April 1910. [St Vigeans gravestone]

ALEXANDER, JOHN, gamekeeper at Kinnaird by Brechin, was accused of mobbing and rioting in the High Street of Brechin in 1830. [NRS.AD14.30.89]

ALEXANDER, JOHN, a sailor aboard the Friendship of Dundee at the Davis Straits in 1824. [NRS.E508.130.8]

ALISON, ROBERT, a Customs officer/Land surveyor in Dundee 1820, who died on 7 November 1855, father of Robert Alison who settled in New South Wales, Australia, before 1859. [NRS.S/H][NRS.E504.11.21]

ALLAN, ALEXANDER, master of the Norval of Dundee in 1816, [NRS.CE70.1.14]

ALLAN, ANDREW, sailor aboard the Princess Charlotte of Dundee bound for the Davis Strait in 1824. [NRS.E508.129.8]

ALLAN, DAVID, sailor aboard the <u>Princess Charlotte of Dundee</u> bound for the Davis Strait in 1824. [NRS.E508.129.8]

ALLAN, GEORGE, was admitted as a weaver burgess of Arbroath in 1797. [AA.18.941]

ALLAN, JOHN, born 1735, a wigmaker in Dundee, died in 1804. [Howff gravestone, Dundee]

ALLAN, ROBERT, master of the <u>Happy Jean of Montrose</u> trading with Norway in 1799. [AJ.2665]

ALLAN, PATRICK, son of John Allan in Arbroath, graduated MA from Marischal College, Aberdeen, in 1812. [MCA]

ALLAN, ROBERT, a merchant in Arbroath, a tack, 1840. [NRS.GD45.16]

ALLAN, WILLIAM, born 1744, 'late of Jamaica', died in 1818, husband of Mary Shanks, born 1768, died 1852. [Arbroath Abbey gravestone]

ALLAN, WILLIAM, from Forfar, graduated MA from King's College, Aberdeen, in March 1837. [KCA]

ALLAN, WILLIAM, from Montrose, graduated MA from King's College, Aberdeen, in March 1858, later minister of Mochrum. [KCA]

ALLARDICE, CHARLOTTE, of Murlingden, Angus, married George Colquhoun Hamilton of Bardownie, Canada West, on 20 March 1855. [EEC.22728]

ALLARDYCE, DAVID, of Memus, a merchant in Brechin, testament, 1793, Comm. Brechin. [NRS]

ALLARDYCE, JAMES, in St Vincent in the British West Indies, married Susanna Keith, daughter of James Keith the Excise Collector of Dundee, there on 1 November 1796. [SM.58.791]

ALLARDYCE, JEAN, widow of James Allardyce a weaver in Brechin, testament, 1792, Comm. Brechin. [NRS]

ALLARDYCE, JOHN, born 1791, a butcher in Pyot's Close, Forfar, was accused of the culpable homicide of John Dempster in Dunnichen in 1836. [NRS.AD14.36.96]

ALLARDYCE, ROBERT, of Memus, a merchant in Brechin, testament, 1793, Comm. Brechin. [NRS]

ALLARDYCE, Dr WILLIAM, in Brechin, a witness to a deed of James Lowe a sugar planter in Trinidad in 1809. [NRS.RD3.315.571]

AMBROSE, CHRISTIAN, born 1744, died 1803, wife of James Robertson, born 1751, a sailor, died 1778. [Howff gravestone, Dundee]

ANDERSON, ALEXANDER, born 1810, son of John Anderson, [1780-1851], and his wife Ann White, [1780-1876], died in New York on 18 December 1845. [Montrose gravestone]

ANDERSON, ALEXANDER, son of James Anderson a farmer in Logie Pert, a student at Marischal College, Aberdeen, in 1820s. [MCA]

ANDERSON, ALEXANDER, a sailor aboard the Dorothy of Dundee bound for the Davis Straits in 1825. [NRS.E508.130.8]

ANDERSON, DAVID, a merchant and shoemaker in Dundee, testament, 1793, Comm. Brechin. [NRS]

ANDERSON, DAVID, a merchant, later a cotton manufacturer in Dundee in 1793. [DCA.B19.2.27/228]

ANDERSON, DAVID, only son of David Anderson, a merchant in Dundee, died in Curacao, Dutch West Indies, on 30 November 1807, on his arrival there from Monte Video, Uruguay. [SM.70.317]

ANDERSON, DAVID, born 1794 in Dundee, died in Riga, Latvia, on 28 September 1834. [Riga gravestone]

ANDERSON, DAVID, born 1798, a farmer who emigrated via Dundee on the brig Traveller bound for Charleston, South Carolina, in 1822. [NRS.E504.11.22][NARA]

ANDERSON, DAVID, steersman aboard the Princess Charlotte of Dundee bound for the Davis Strait in 1824. [NRS.E508.129.8]

ANDERSON, DAVID, son of Thomas Anderson a farmer in Panbride, a student at Marischal College, Aberdeen, in1830s. [MCA]

ANDERSON, DAVID, an engineer from Angus, married Phillis Irving from Annan, in New York in 1857. [Annandale Observer]

ANDERSON, DUNCAN, sailor aboard the Estridge of Dundee bound for the Davis Straits in 1824. [NRS.E508.129.8]

ANDERSON, FRANCIS, born 1737, son of Francis Anderson and his wife Ann Smith, farmer in Broadfold, Rescobie, died 13 December 1802. [Rescobie gravestone]

ANDERSON, GEORGE, a writer in Brechin, died 1 December 1824, an inventory, 1827. [NRS.GD45.18.1119]

ANDERSON, GEORGE, servant to James Hunter a farmer in Kettins, was accused of housebreaking in 1828. [NRS.AD14.28.245]

ANDERSON, GEORGE, son of Thomas Anderson a farmer in Panbride, a student at Marischal College, Aberdeen in 1844. [MCA]

ANDERSON, HENDRY, born 1724, tenant in Greenford, died in 1794, husband of Elisabeth Sutter. [Arbirlot gravestone]

ANDERSON, HENRY, a sailor aboard the whaler Mary Ann of Dundee from Dundee to Greenland on 4 March 1813, abandoned the ship on return at Aberdeen to avoid the Press Gang on 16 August 1813. [NRS.E508.115.8]

ANDERSON, JAMES, in Wormyhills, Arbirlot, in 1799. [NRS.GD45.18.2012]

ANDERSON, JAMES, from Angus, graduated MA from King's College, Aberdeen, on 25 March 1808. [KCA]

ANDERSON, JAMES, son of William Anderson an auctioneer in Kirriemuir, a student at Marischal College, Aberdeen, in 1820s, later minister of the Original Secession Church in Kirriemuir. [MCA]

ANDERSON, JAMES ROBERT, son of Thomas Anderson a farmer in Panbride, a student at Marischal College, Aberdeen, in 1843. [MCA]

ANDERSON, JAMES, third son of James Anderson a wine merchant in Arbroath, died in New York on 1 November 1868. [S.7897]

ANDERSON, JEAN, born 1730, died in 1823, wife of Alexander Myers, [1720-1786], a carrier burgess of Montrose. [Montrose gravestone]

ANDERSON, JOHN, [1788-1860], and his wife Elizabeth Lindsay, parents of David Anderson, John Anderson, and William Anderson, who all died in Australia. [Forfar gravestone]

ANDERSON, JOHN, in the Mill of Auchterhouse, was the victim of a culpable homicide in 1836. [NRS.AD14.36.89]

ANDERSON, JOHN, in Smithfield, Dundee, an officer of the law, was assaulted in Trottick in 1837. [NRS.AD14.37.123]

ANDERSON, PATRICK, in Westhaven of Panbride, testament, 1796, Comm. Brechin. [NRS]

ANDERSON, PATRICK PROCTOR, born 1809, town clerk of Ipswich, Queensland, Australia, died 26 January 1869. [Arbroath Abbey gravestone]

ANDERSON, PETER, tenant famer of Broadfaulds, Guthrie, 1856. [AVR]

ANDERSON, ROBERT, master of the <u>Dundee of Dundee</u> in 1809. [DD]

ANDERSON, ROBERT, from Montrose, a merchant in Sydney, Australia, by 1843. [NRS.S/H]

ANDERSON, THOMAS, born 1795, son of George Anderson and his wife Agnes Kerr in Inverkeillor, died in New Orleans, Louisiana, on 1 August 1835. [Inverkeillor gravestone]

ANDERSON, THOMAS, son of Thomas Anderson a farmer in Panbride, a student at Marischal College, Aberdeen in 1844. [MCA]

ANDERSON, WILLIAM, born 1805, of Brown Street, Dundee, was accused of robbing, rioting and assaulting army officers at Dudhope Barracks, Dundee, in 1832. [NRS.AD14.32.29]

ANDERSON, Captain, master of the <u>Hector of Dundee</u> from the River Clyde to Pictou, Nova Scotia, in 1843. [GA.5903]

ANDSON, JOHN, a merchant in Arbroath, died 1814. [SLH.105]

ANGUS, JOHN, MA in 1796, was granted a Doctor of Laws degree by Marischal College, in 1811, a patron of the Aberdeen Society who collected funds in India. [MCA]

ARCHER, JAMES, born 1800, son of James Archer and his wife Jean Dargie, a mariner who died in Melbourne, Australia, on 24 February 1854. [Monifieth gravestone]

ARCHER, Reverend JAMES, born 1801, son of Andrew Archer, [1769-1823], died in New Lebanon, Montgomery County, Ohio, in 1825. [Tealing gravestone]

ARCHER, JAMES, a skipper in Fish Street, Dundee, in 1818. [DD]

ARCHIBALD, ROBERT, born 1802 in Dundee, an accountant in the Honourable East India Company Mint, died on 14 May 1832, [South Park gravestone, Calcutta, India]

ARKLEY, EVELYN, daughter of Patrick Arkley and his wife Julia, died in Lynn, Massachusetts, in 1869. [Murroes gravestone]

ARKLAY, JOHN, son of John Arklay a merchant in Brechin, a student at Marischal College, Aberdeen, in 1820s. [MCA]

ARKLAY, PETER, of Dunninald, died there on 31 December 1825. [SM.97.255]

ARKLAY, WILLIAM, in Wellgate, Dundee, master of the <u>Alexander</u> in 1818. [DD]

ARTHUR, Captain JAMES, born 1798, son of .... Arthur and his wife Elizabeth Herald, died in New York in April 1838. [St Andrew's gravestone, Dundee]

AYRE, ROBERT MACKENZIE, born 1827, son of William Ayre and his wife Agnes Gordon, died in Benduck Hay, New South Wales, Australia, on 2 November 1892, [Brechin Cathedral gravestone]

BAILLIE, JAMES, born 1812, son of William Baillie and his wife Jean Kydd, died in Melbourne, Australia, on 2 December 1854. [Arbroath Abbey gravestone]

BAILLIE, JAMES, junior, a weaver in Cadger's Wynd, Brechin, was accused of mobbing and rioting in the High Street of Brechin in 1830. [NRS.AD14.30.89]

BAILLIE, WILLIAM, a writer in Montrose in 1779, died in 1805, husband of Margaret Kennedy who died in 1797. Witness to a deed of James Cruickshank of Richmond, St Vincent, in 1793. [NRS.RD4.270.1097] [NRS.E326.3.19][Montrose gravestone]

BAIN, WALTER, a mason in Wellgate, Dundee, in 1796. [DCA.B19.3.26/1]

BALFOUR, ALEXANDER, a shoemaker in Montrose, testament, 1800, Comm. Brechin. [NRS]

BALFOUR, JAMES, born 1822, a flaxdresser of 39 Barn Green, Arbroath, died 10 June 1884, husband of Margaret Cornal, born 1817, died 12 October 1893. [St Vigeans gravestone]

BALFOUR, JOHN, tenant in Shelly, Lochlee, testament, 1799, Comm. Brechin. [NRS]

BALFOUR, WILLIAM, a vintner in Carnoustie, a tack, 1840. [NRS.GD45.16]

BAND, DAVID, steersman aboard the Dorothy of Dundee bound for the Davis Straits in 1825. [NRS.E508.130.8]

BANKS, GEORGE, master of the Fame of Dundee in 1825. [DSR]

BANKS, JAMES, sailor aboard the Estridge of Dundee bound for the Davis Straits in 1824. [NRS.E508.129.8]

BARCLAY, ALEXANDER, born 1711, from Dundee, emigrated in 1726, settled in Amelia County, Virginia, died 22 October 1825. [Virginia Genealogist, 6.169]

BARCLAY, JAMES, born 1790 in Montrose, died in Bermuda on 11 March 1831, buried in St Peter's, parish of St George, Bermuda. [Bermuda gravestone]

BARCLAY, ROBERT, son of David Barclay in Logie Pert, graduated MA from Marischal College, Aberdeen, in 1802, later minister at Lunan. [MCA]

BARCLAY, ROBERT, master of the Agnes from Dundee to Kingston, Jamaica, on 24 April 1819. [NRS.E504.11.21]

BARKER, JAMES, was admitted as a weaver burgess of Arbroath in 1797. [AA.18.941]

BARRACK, ALEXANDER, son of Alexander Barrack in Forfar, graduated MA from Marischal College, Aberdeen, in 1817. [MCA]

BARRIE, THOMAS, a mariner and weaver in Hilltown, Dundee, accused of theft from the Thomas of Dundee in Dundee harbour in 1837. [NRS.AD14.37.117]

BARRON, ANDREW, in St Clement's Lane, Dundee, master of the Mary Anne of Dundee in 1818. [DSR]; trading between Memel, Lithuania, and Dundee in 1819. [NRS.E504.11.21]

BARRON, JAMES, master of the Abeona of Dundee trading between Libau, Latvia, and Dundee in 1818. [NRS.E504.11.21]; master of the Margaret of Dundee, trading between Russia and Dundee in 1831. [MD.117]

BATHIE, GEORGE, husband of Helen Smith born 1776 who died 15 December 1829, son George Bathie born 1833, died 11 March 1855. [Murroes gravestone]

BATLEY, MARY, from Glamis, died in Toronto, Ontario, on 9 August 1849. [EEC.21879]

BATTHY, MARY, born 20 June 1811, daughter of Andrew Batthy a labourer, born in Dundee, and his wife Helen Laird, daughter of Thomas Laird, a weaver born in Kirriemuir, was baptised in the Qualified Episcopal Chapel in Dundee on 28 June 1811. [DE.7]

BAULD, ANDREW, a merchant in Arbroath in 1796. [NRS.CS230.Seqn.B1.15]

BAXTER, ALEXANDER, born 1723, died 1796, husband of Margaret Mitchell, born 1734, died 1801. [Howff gravestone, Dundee]

BAXTER, DAVID, master of the Peggy of Dundee, trading between Riga, Latvia, and Dundee in 1796. [NRS.CE70.1.8/4]; master of the Chance of Dundee in 1809. [DD]

BAXTER, DAVID, a farmer and leather merchant in Kirriemuir, 1842. [NRS.CS280.4/5]

BAXTER, EDMOND, son of a merchant in Dundee, a student at Marischal College, Aberdeen, in 1820s. [MCA]

BAXTER, ELISABETH, born 1763, died 1798, wife of John Waddel a maltman in Dundee. [Howff gravestone, Dundee]

BAXTER, JOHN, an apprentice to George Deuchars master of the brig Jean of Dundee, was accused of mobbing and rioting in 1816. [NRS.AD14.16.58]

BAXTER, PETER, in Crosston of Aberlemno, was accused of the murder of James Lindsay in Letham, Dunnichen, in 1831, found guilty and imprisoned for 12 months. [NRS.AD14.32.24; JC26.1832.306]

BAXTER, WILLIAM LINTON, from Dundee, graduated MA from King's College, Aberdeen, in March 1856, later minister at Careston. [KCA]

BEATTIE, ELIZABETH, in Montrose, was accused of mobbing and rioting there in 1813. [NRS.AD14.13.84]

BEATTIE, JAMES, son of James Beattie a farmer in Inverkeilor, a student at Marischal College, Aberdeen, around 1818. [MCA]

BEATTIE, WILLIAM, born 1773, a shipmaster in Arbroath, died in 1816. [Arbroath Abbey gravestone]

BEGG, JAMES, born 24 September 1814 in Dundee, son of ...... Begg and his wife Margaret Ramsay, emigrated to Quebec on 1 April 1827, settled in Glengarry County, Upper Canada. [CSG.28]

BEIG, ALEXANDER, born 1737, a manufacturer in Hilltown, Dundee, died 1819, husband of Catherine Thom, born 1752, died in 1785. [Howff gravestone, Dundee]

BELL, ALEXANDER, born 1770, a shipmaster in Dundee, died in 1808. [Howff gravestone, Dundee]

BELL, ANDREW, born 1755, son of William Bell a shipmaster, a burgess of Dundee in 1777, master of the Riga Merchant of Dundee, trading between Archangel, Russia, and Dundee in 1794, [NRS.CE70.1.8/90]; master of the Despatch of Dundee in 1797, and of the Robert and Mary of Dundee in 1809, died in 1827. [NRS.CE70.1.8/77][Howff gravestone, Dundee][DBR][DD]

BELL, DAVID, born 1817, son of Alexander Bell, a surgeon, and his wife Anne Ruthven Leven, a coffee planter who died in Kandy, Ceylon, on 26 September 1849. [Howff, Dundee]

BELL, JAMES, a merchant in Arbroath, a trustee in 1791. [NRS.CS96.2037]

BELL, JAMES, a rope and sailmaker in Dundee, re an assignation of land in Newton Panbride, 1840. [NRS.GD45.16.2155]

BELL, JOHN, from Dundee, died on Crescent Estate, Jamaica, on 9 March 1803. [EA.4117.03]

BELL, Reverend PATRICK, born 12 May 1799 in Auchterhouse, was educated at the University of St Andrews, minister at Carmyllie, inventor of the reaping machine, died 22 April 1869. [AA]

BELL, PETER, a farmer in Cransley, parish of Lundie and Foulis, victim of an armed robbery in 1840. [NRS.AD14.40.295]

BELL, SAMUEL, born 1740, an architect, died in 1813. [Howff gravestone, Dundee]

BELL, WILLIAM, master of the Riga Merchant of Dundee trading between Archangel, Russia, and Dundee, in 1794. [NRS.CE70.1.8/90]

BENNET, PETER, a flax dresser in Overgait, Dundee, was accused of mobbing and rioting in the New Hall, Bell Street, Dundee, in 1842. [NRS.AD14.42.354; JC26.1843.443]

BERRIE, JAMES, master of the Victoria of Dundee from Dundee to Montreal in 1832, 1834, 1835. [DPCA]

BERTIE, JAMES, a manufacturer in Almerie Close, Arbroath, sederunt book, 1813-1815. [NRS.CS96.881]

BETTS, JAMES, master of the Unity of Dundee, lost at sea between Stettin, Germany, and Dundee in 1841. [MD.148]

BIRNIE, DAVID, a merchant and flax spinner at Witch's Know, Dundee, versus Charles Fenton, a heckler in Dundee, 1811. [NRS.CS36.2.31]

BIRRELL, MARGARET, daughter of Robert Birrell a shipmaster in Dundee, testament, 1795, Comm. Brechin. [NRS]

BISSET, ANDREW, son of Andrew Bisset an inspector in Montrose, a student at Marischal College, Aberdeen around 1820, graduated MA from Cambridge in 1839, a barrister of Lincoln's Inn, London. [MCA]

BISSET, STURROCK, line manager of the Friendship of Dundee at the Davis Straits in 1824. [NRS.E508.130.8]

BISSET, WILLIAM, a merchant in Dundee in 1798. [DCA.B19.3.27/8]

BLACK, ALEXANDER, a bookseller, married Hellen Duncan, third daughter of Robert Duncan a merchant in Brechin, there on 16 December 1825. [SM.97.126]

BLACK, CHARLES, born in Brechin, a flax spinner and blacksmith at Douglaston Spinning Mill, Kinnettles, was accused of assault in 1826. [NRS.AD14.26.178]

BLACK, DAVID C., a shipmaster from Arbroath, settled in Alexandria, Virginia, before 1820. [UNC.Black pp.2530]

BLACK, DAVID DAKERS, a rent collector in Careston, 1834. [NRS.CS46.834.2/3]

BLACK, DAVID, a tenant grazier and cattle dealer in Brechin, 1844. [NRS.CS280.6.7]

BLACK, ISABELLA, wife of David Black in Inverarity, a victim of a mob and rioters in the New Hall, Bell Street, Dundee, in 1842. [NRS.AD14.42.354; JC26.1843.443]

BLACK, JAMES, at Barrelwell, Brechin, a farmer and distiller 1844. [NRS.CS280.6.8]

BLACK, JOHN, was admitted as a merchant burgess of Arbroath in 1798. [AA.18.941]

BLACK, JOHN, born 1791, a labourer from Lundy, emigrated via Greenock aboard the William of New York bound for New York on 4 September 1817, arrived there on 17 October 1817. [NY Commercial Advertiser, 18.10.1817]

BLACK, PETER, a weaver on Fauldy Hill, Panbride, a tack, 1840. [NRS.GD45.16]

BLACK, Captain, master of the Amelia of Dundee which was shored at Narva, Russia, in 1843. [MD.157]

BLACKADDER, WILLIAM, a surveyor in Glamis, records, 1813-1841. [NRS.GD362.9-28]

BLACKIE, ELIZABETH, wife of David Paterson a sailor in Montrose, was accused of mobbing and rioting there in 1813. [NRS.AD14.13.84]

BLAIR, HOMER, son of Reverend David Blair in Brechin, died in Savanna-la-Mar, Westmoreland, Jamaica, in 1817. [S.2.60]

BLAIR, JAMES, son of David Blair in Ploverhilloch of Dunbarrow, Dunnichen, was accused of assault in 1833. [NRS.AD14.33.84]

BLAIR, JOHN, in Charlestown, America, heir to his aunt Agnes Blair, daughter of Reverend George Blair in Edzell in 1806. [NRS.S/H]

BLAIR, JOHN, sailor aboard the Princess Charlotte of Dundee bound for the Davis Strait in 1824. [NRS.E508.129.8]

BLUES, ALEXANDER, in Nethergait, Dundee, in 1818, master of the Mayflower of Dundee in 1809, and the Juno of Dundee. [DD]

BLUES, JOHN, a shipmaster in Montrose, who died on 9 Jun 1851, uncle of Jane, Margaret, and Rebecca Blues in Tagenrog, Russia. [NRS.S/H.1880]

BLYTH, ALEXANDER, born 1832, James Blyth, born 1840, and William Blyth, born 1829, sons of David Blyth and his wife Martha Cuthbert, Alexander died in Winton, New Zealand, on 9 March 1901, James died in Invercargill, N.Z., on 30 November 1892, and William died in Christchurch, N.Z., in 1898. [Kinnell gravestone]

BLYTH, DAVID, harpooner aboard the Dorothy, was drowned at Dundee in March 1828. [HS.18.1.19]

BLYTH, ROBERT, born 1840, an engineer who died in Calcutta, India, on 3 May 1869. [Western gravestone, Dundee]

BOATH, JAMES, was admitted as a weaver burgess of Arbroath in 1797. [AA.18.941]

BOATH, JOHN, was admitted as a weaver burgess of Arbroath in 1797. [AA.18.941]

BONELLA, JAMES H., born 1791 a surgeon in Carnoustie, died 20 September 1875, husband of Elizabeth Gibson, born 1810, died 12 August 1871. [Barry gravestone]

BORTHWICK, CHARLES, born 1840, son of James Borthwick and his wife Mary Milne, died in San Francisco, California, on 12 August 1881. [Arbroath Abbey gravestone] [NRS.S/H.]

BOSWELL, ROBERT, was admitted as a burgess of Arbroath in 1795. [AA.18.941]

BOWACK, PETER, born 1807, a flax dresser of Wardmill Croft, Arbroath, was accused of theft in 1824. [NRS.AD14.24.110]

BOWER, ALEXANDER, of Kincaldrum, trustee of the lands of Glaswell, Kirriemuir, in 1803. [NRS.CS230.L.5.3]

BOWER, JAMES, and his wife Anne Anderson, parents of Alexander Bower, born 1859, an electrical engineer, died in Melbourne, Australia, on 23 October 1887. [Inverkeillor gravestone]

BOWER, ROBERT, a farmer, grazier and cattle dealer in Meathie in 1842. [NRS.CS280.9.5]

BOWER, WILLIAM, in Arbroath, exported a cargo of linen on the Laurel, Captain Spink, from Dundee to Kingston, Jamaica, in October 1820. [NRS.E504.11.21]

BOWERS, Captain, master of the Henry of Montrose trading between Montrose and Quebec from 1849 to 1854. [LCL][EEC]

BOWES, MARGARET, wife of James Gray a tenant in Pitkerro, testament, 1791, Comm. Brechin. [NRS]

BOWES, MARGARET, in Lethnot, testament, 1792, Comm. Brechin. [NRS]

BOWMAN, GEORGE, a burgess of Dundee in 1781, [DBR]; a skipper on the Shore, Dundee, in 1782, and in the Nethergait, Dundee, in 1809, [DD]; husband of Alison Pattullo, 1799. [DCA.B19.3.27/172]

BOWMAN, JAMES, master of the Noah of Dundee in 1809. [DD]

BOWMAN, WILLIAM, born 1800, a blacksmith in Bridgeton, died in September 1865. [St Vigeans gravestone]

BOYACK, DAVID, born 1784, died in Kingston, Jamaica, on 25 June 1820, Howff gravestone, Dundee]

BOYD, ALEXANDER, sr., a weaver, at the West Port, Dundee, and Alexander Boyd jr a labourer there, were accused of theft in 1830. [NRS.AD14.30.90; JC26.1830.17]

BOYICK, JOHN, born 1745, a shoemaker in Montrose, died in 1810, husband of Ann Allardice, born 1738, died 1819. [Montrose gravestone]

BOYS, HENRY, in Forfar, graduated MD from King's College, Aberdeen, on 20 May 1805. [KCA]

BOYTER, DAVID, a shipmaster in Dundee, testament, 1792, Comm. Brechin. [NRS]

BOYTER, GEORGE, a sailor aboard the Friendship of Dundee at the Davis Straits in 1824. [NRS.E508.130.8]

BOYTER, ROBERT, a sailor of the Friendship of Dundee at the Davis Straits in 1824. [NRS.E508.130.8]

BRAICK, DAVID, son of John Braick a merchant in Arbroath, graduated MA from Marischal College in 1813. [MCA]

BRAID, JAMES, surgeon aboard the Dorothy of Dundee at the Davis Straits in 1824. [NRS.E508.130.8]

BRAND, ALEXANDER, in London, was admitted as a burgess of Arbroath in 1790. [AA.18.941]

BRAND, JAMES, in London, was admitted as a burgess of Arbroath in 1790. [AA.18.941]

BRAND, WILLIAM, born in October 1813 in Dundee, son of James Brand and his wife Isabella Nicoll, a merchant in New York from 1841 to 1865, died near Dundee on 11 December 1882. [ANY]

BREMNER, JOHN, was admitted as a weaver burgess of Arbroath in 1797. [AA.18.941]

BRODIE, GEORGE, was admitted as a writer burgess of Arbroath in 1797. [AA.18.941]

BRODIE, JOHN, born 1799 in Dundee, son of John Brodie and his wife Elizabeth Archibald, emigrated to USA in 1819, a slater in New York, married Helen Pirnie on 2 January 1835, died in New York in 1866. [ANY]

BROWN, ALEXANDER, was admitted as a weaver burgess of Arbroath in 1797. [AA.18.941]

BROWN, ALEXANDER, a shipmaster in Fish Street, Dundee, in 1818, master of the Jean of Dundee in 1817-1818, [NRS.E504.11.20], master of the Alert in 1818, master of the Armistead of Dundee in 1825, [DSR]; testament, 1840, [NRS.SC45.31.5.319]

BROWN, CHARLES, a skipper in Fish Street, Dundee, and master of the Sparkler of Dundee in 1809, and master of the Nelson in 1818. [DD]

BROWN, DAVID, was admitted as a weaver burgess of Arbroath in 1797. [AA.18.941]

BROWN, ELSPETH, wife of Andrew Petrie in Craigmill, testament, 1791, Comm. Brechin. [NRS]

BROWN, GEORGE, born 1842, son of David Brown and his wife Ann Johnston, died in Sydney, Australia, on 9 May 1879. [Arbroath Abbey gravestone]

BROWN, JAMES, a skipper in the Vault, Dundee, in 1782, and on Windmill Brae, Dundee, in 1809, [DD]; master of the Alert of Dundee in 1796, [NRS.CE70.1.8/70]

BROWN, JAMES HODGE, born 1830, son of William Brown and his wife Jean Hodge, died in Auckland, New Zealand, on 1 November 1861. [Eastern Necropolis gravestone, Dundee]

BROWN, JOHN, a merchant in Dundee, testament, 1794, Comm. Brechin. [NRS]

BROWN, JOHN, a ship carpenter in Dundee, testament, 1796, Comm. Brechin. [NRS]

BROWN, LAWRENCE, from Dundee, a merchant in St Petersburg, Russia, in 1803. [NRS.S/H]

BROWN, MARGARET, in Dundee, widow of James McRobie, testament, 1799, Comm. Brechin. [NRS]

BROWN, PATRICK, feuar in Blackscroft, Dundee, testament, 1793, Comm. Brechin. [NRS]

BROWN, PATRICK, apprentice to the Town Clerk of Dundee in 1796. [DCA.B19.3.26/7]

BROWN, PATRICK, born 1778, died in India on 25 June 1811. [Howff gravestone, Dundee]

BROWN, THOMAS, a shipmaster in Dundee, testament, 1792, Comm. Brechin. [NRS]

BROWN, WILLIAM, from Forfar, graduated MA from King's College, Aberdeen, in March 1818. [KCA]

BRUCE, DAVID, born 1740, a shipmaster in Dundee, died in 1803. [Howff gravestone, Dundee]

BRUCE, JAMES S., a surgeon in Brechin, and his brother David Bruce, an account, 1823. [NRS.GD45.31.422]

BRUCE, JAMES, born 1840, was lost in New Zealand on 2 September 1870. [Howff gravestone, Dundee]

BRUCE, JOHN, son of Reverend Bruce in Forfar, graduated MA from Marischal College in 1812. [MCA]

BRUCE, MARGARET, widow of Colin Bruce of Seaforth, died at Windmill House, Arbroath, on 7 December 1825. [SM.97.128]

BRUCE, WILLIAM, son of Reverend William Bruce in Arbroath, a student in Marischal College in 1790s. [MCA]

BUCHAN, DAVID OGILVIE, son of John Buchan an Episcopal minister in Kirriemuir, a student at Marischal College, Aberdeen, in 1827. [MCA]

BUCHAN, ROBERT, a merchant, was granted a tack in Slateford, Edzell, in 1838. [NRS.GD45.16.1917]

BUCHANAN, JAMES, late of St Thomas in the West Indies, was admitted as a burgess of Montrose in 1783. [MBR]

BURGESS, THEO, master of the Eliza of Dundee in 1809. [NARA. Mf.237]

BURMAN, JAMES, in Newtyle, sequestration, 1815. [NRS.CS236.B20.1]

BURMAN, JESSIE, born 1824, daughter of James Burman and his wife Cecilia Clark, widow of Reverend John Gow, died in Carmyllie, Touranga, Upotiki, New Zealand, on 17 November 1906. [Newtyle gravestone]

BURMAN, PETER, born 1814, son of James Burman and his wife Cecilia Clark, a writer who died in Australia in 1841. [Newtyle gravestone]

BURN, ELIZABETH, in Montrose, was accused of mobbing and rioting there in 1813. [NRS.AD14.13.84]

BURN, JAMES, town clerk of Montrose, a letter, 1838. [NRS.GD45.14.633]

BURNS, WILLIAM, in Arbroath, exported a cargo of linen on the Laurel, Captain Spink, from Dundee to Kingston, Jamaica, in October 1820. [NRS.E504.11.21]

BURNET, DAVID, a farmer in Kirriemuir, was accused of assaulting officers of the law, later failed to appear in court and was outlawed in 1827. [NRS.JC26.1827.5]

BURNET, JAMES, born 1770, was admitted as a weaver burgess of Arbroath in 1794, died on 28 May 1807, husband of Jean Strachan. [AA.18.941] [Arbroath Abbey gravestone]

BURNET, THOMAS, a crofter in Airlie, was accused of assaulting officers of the law, later failed to appear in court and was outlawed in 1827. [NRS.JC26.1827.5]

BURNS, WILLIAM, was admitted as a carter burgess of Arbroath in 1797. [AA.18.941]

BURNS, WILLIAM, from Forfar, graduated MA from King's College, Aberdeen, in March 1835. [KCA]

BUTCHART, ALEXANDER, was admitted as a manufacturer burgess of Arbroath in 1797. [AA.18.941]

BUTCHART, JAMES, a journeyman carpenter, son of James Butchart a confectioner in Dundee, was accused of assault in 1819. [NRS.AD14.19.167]

BUTCHART, JOHN, a timber merchant in Quebec, only son of Andrew Butchart a shipmaster in Arbroath, a deed dated 1819, another dated 1821. [NRS.RD5.150.10; RD5.198.295]

BUTCHART, JOHN, born 1772, a mason In Carnoustie, died 13 February 1847, husband of Agnes Anderson, born 1773, died 11 December 1835. [Barry gravestone]

BUTCHART, ROBERT, was admitted as a manufacturer burgess of Arbroath in 1797. [AA.18.941]

BUTCHART, ROBERT, a wright in Arbirlot, a tack, 1840. [NRS.GD45.16.1732]; a notebook, [NRS.GD1.1248.1]

BUTCHART, WILLIAM, was admitted as a manufacturer burgess of Arbroath in 1797. [AA.18.941]

BUTTAR, JOHN, sailor aboard the Princess Charlotte of Dundee bound for the Davis Strait in 1824. [NRS.E508.129.8]

BUTTER, THOMAS, born 1746, a merchant in the West Port of Dundee, died 1825, husband of Janet McIntosh, born 1745, died 1818. [Howff gravestone, Dundee]

BUTTAR, WILLIAM, a fresh or green man aboard the Dorothy of Dundee bound for the Davis Straits in 1825. [NRS.E508.130.8]

BUTTERWORTH, MICHAEL, a haberdasher in Dundee, sederunt book, 1819-1820. [NRS.CS96.320]

CABEL, JAMES, born 1741, a shipmaster in Dundee, died in 1814. [Howff gravestone, Dundee]

CABEL, JAMES, the younger, a skipper in Seagait, Dundee, in 1809, master of the William of Dundee in 1795, [NRS.CE70.1.8/58]; testament, 1833. [NRS.SC45.31.1.226]

CAIRD, ALEXANDER, a skipper in Fish Street, Dundee, in 1809, 1818, [DD]; master of the Isabella of Dundee in 1795, [NRS.CE70.1.8/7]; master of the Baltic of Dundee in1809, and of the Ruby in 1818. [DD]; master of the Smart trading between Dundee and Riga, Latvia, in February 1820. [NRS.E504.11.21]

CAIRD, JAMES, was admitted as a weaver burgess of Arbroath in 1797. [AA.18.941]; his widow Jean Campbell, testament, 1799, Comm. St Andrews. [NRS]

CAIRD, JOHN, was admitted as a confectioner burgess of Arbroath in 1793. [AA.18.941]

CAIRD, JOHN L., son of John Caird, [1794-1863], and his wife Ann Lumgair, [1796-1860], died in Kumaru, New Zealand, on 30 September 1882. [Arbroath Abbey gravestone]

CAIRNCROSS, DAVID, a mariner in Broughty Ferry, testament, 1812. [NRS.CC3]

CAIRNCROSS, JAMES, born 1786, from Carnoustie, a minister in Birsay, from 1818 to 1842, emigrated to Wisconsin, died in Blandford on 23 November 1851. [Annals of the Original Secession Church.541]

CAIRNCROSS, JOHN, a tenant farmer in Camp Farm, Monifieth, accused of housebreaking and theft in 1824. [NRS.AD14.24.95]

CAIRNCROSS, ROBERT, and his wife Janet Gowans, parents of John Cairncross, born 25 May 1827, died in Melbourne, Australia, on 15 January 1858. [Brechin Cathedral gravestone]

CAIRNS, DAVID, sailor aboard the Estridge of Dundee bound for the Davis Straits in 1824. [NRS.E508.129.8]

CAIRNS, JAMES, master of the James and David of Dundee in 1809. [DD]

CAIRY, DAVID, was admitted as a burgess of Arbroath in 1795. [AA.18.941]

CAITHNESS, CHARLES, a shipmaster in Dundee, father of Margaret Caithness or Ulich in Norway, and Mary Caithness in Ask, Norway, 1831. [NRS.S/H]

CAITHNESS, DAVID, master of the Curlew of Dundee in 1809. [DD]

CAITHNESS, DAVID, line manager aboard the Estridge of Dundee, for the Davis Straits in 1824. [NRS.E508.129.8]

CAITHNESS, GEORGE, born 1730, a shipmaster in Broughty Ferry, died 19 February 1801, husband of Agnes Lyall, father of George Caithness a shipmaster. [Broughty Ferry gravestone]

CAITHNESS, GEORGE, master of the Albion of Dundee in 1809. [DD]; master of the Laurel of Dundee trading between Danzig, Prusssia, and Dundee in 1819. [NRS.E504.11.21]

CAITHNESS, JAMES, born 1781, husband of Janet Henry, died on 11 August 1808, [Broughty Ferry gravestone]; master of the Peggy of Dundee in 1798, and of the David and Jean of Dundee in 1799. [NRS.CE70.1.8], master of the Duchess of Athole in 1809. [DD]

CAITHNESS, JOHN, master of the Margaret and Betsy of Dundee in 1809, [DD]; a skipper in Westhaven of Panbride, testament, 1823. [NRS.CC3]

CAMERON, JAMES WATSON, from Dundee, a merchant in New York during the 1840s, settled on Staten Island, N.Y., possibly died in Dundee. [ANY]

CAMERON, JESSIE, born 1827, daughter of William Cameron and his wife Mary Eils, died in Australia on 30 May 1862. [Lundie gravestone]

CAMERON, JOHN, a labourer in Lydiat, Lundie, was accused of theft in 1835. [NRS.AD14.141.2]

CAMERON, ROBERT, harpooner aboard the Princess Charlotte of Dundee bound for the Davis Strait in 1824. [NRS.E508.129.8]

CAMPBELL, ALEXANDER, an innkeeper in Kirriemuir, was found guilty of assault and imprisoned in Forfar for six months in 1827. [NRS.JC26.1827.17]

CAMPBELL, JOHN, at the East Port of Forfar, was accused of housebreaking at Balgavies, Aberlemno, in 1830. [NRS.AD14.30.56; JC26.1830.16]

CAMPBELL, WILLIAM, born 1823, married, a carter in Stobsmuir, Dundee, was accused of assault in 1847. [NRS.AD14.47.71]

CANT, JAMES, was admitted as a baker burgess of Arbroath in 1795. [AA.18.941]

CANT, THOMAS, was admitted as a cabinet-maker burgess of Arbroath in 1797. [AA.18.941]

CARDNO, JAMES, an earthenware dealer in Montrose in June 1839. [NRS.CS46.1839.6/12]

CAREY, JAMES, a tenant in West Bank, Lochlee, a tack, 1841. [NRS.GD45.16.1922]

CARGILL, DAVID, master of the Bell and Ann of Arbroath in 1798. [AJ.2617]

CARGILL, DAVID LAWSON, born 1781, a shipmaster in Arbroath, died in 1819. [Arbroath Abbey gravestone]

CARGILL, DAVID, from Angus, graduated MA from King's College, Aberdeen, in April 1830, later a missionary in Africa. [KCA]

CARGILL, DAVID DUFFUS, a merchant and flax-spinner in Arbroath, was accused of forgery in 1833. [NRS.AD14.33.31]

CARGILL, JAMES, born 1797, died 11 November 1837, husband of Agnes Eaton, born 1800, died 26 June 1860. [St Vigeans gravestone]

CARGILL, JOHN, born 1765, was admitted as a shipmaster burgess of Arbroath in 1796, died in 1843, husband of Ann Paterson. [AA.18.941] [Arbroath Abbey gravestone]; master of the Jessy Watson of Arbroath trading between Pillau, Germany, and Dundee in 1818. [NRS.E504.11.21]

CARGILL, THOMAS, was admitted as a baker burgess of Arbroath in 1799. [AA.18.941]

CARGILL, WILLIAM, a weaver in Sparrowcroft, Forfar, a victim of theft in 1825. [NRS.AD14.25.244]

CARNEGIE, ELIZABETH, daughter of David Carnegie of Craig, testament, 7 November 1800, Comm. Brechin. [NRS]

CARNEGY, Lady ELIZABETH, daughter of the Earl of Northesk, married Colonel Thackeray of the Royal Engineers, in Hampshire on 24 November 1825. [SM.97.126]

CARNEGIE, GEORGE, was admitted as a burgess of Arbroath in 1793. [AA.18.941]

CARNEGIE, Sir JAMES, of Southesk, married Charlotte Lysons, daughter of Reverend Daniel Lysons of Gloucestershire, in Naples, Italy, on 14 November 1825. [SM.97.126]

CARNEGIE, Reverend JOHN, in Inverkeillor, was admitted as a burgess of Arbroath in 1791. [AA.18.941]

CARNEGIE, JOHN, son of Robert Carnegie in Angus, a student in Marischal College in 1790s. [MCA]

CARNEGIE, JOHN, from Brechin, a student in Marischal College in 1790s. [MCA]

CARNEGY, P. of the estate of Turin, a plan, 1830. [NRS.RHP.15868]

CARNEGIE, Dr STEWART, son of James Carnegie of Balmachie, died in Goshen, Jamaica, on 26 December 1807. [SM.70.317]

CARNEGIE, THOMAS, in Logie Pert, a petition, 1850. [NRS.CR2.72]

CARR, ALEXANDER, a wright, was granted a tack in Slateford, Edzell, in 1838. [NRS.GD45.16.1916]

CARR, ALEXANDER, [1819-1893], and his wife Susan Graham, [1823-1905], parents of John Carr who died in New Zealand on 9 October 1925. [Edzell gravestone]

CARR, WILLIAM, a shoemaker, was granted a tack in Slateford, Edzell, in 1838. [NRS.GD45.16.1920]

CATHRO, JAMES, born 1735, a brewer in Dundee, died in 1799, husband of Elisabeth Patullo, born 1735, died in 1807. [Howff gravestone, Dundee][DCA.B19.3.27/233]

CATHRO, JAMES, a skipper in Crichton Street, Dundee, master of the Livingston of Dundee in 1809. [DD].

CATHRO, KATHERINE, born 1773, died 28 November 1829, wife of Alexander Orem. [Murroes gravestone]

CATHROW, WILLIAM, was admitted as a brewer burgess of Arbroath in 1792. [AA.18.941]

CHALMERS, ALEXANDER, was admitted as a shoe-maker burgess of Arbroath in 1797. [AA.18.941]

CHALMERS, ANDREW, a Lieutenant of the Royal Navy, testament, 26 October 1791, Comm. Brechin. [NRS]

CHALMERS, JAMES, born 2 February 1782 in Arbroath, inventor of the adhesive postage stamp, died in Dundee on 26 May 1853. [St Paul's Cathedral, Dundee, plaque]

CHAPEL, JOHN, born 1745, a ship-owner in Arbroath, died in 1817, husband of Katherine Smith, born 1748, died 1813. [Arbroath Abbey gravestone]

CHAPEL, JOHN, was admitted as a butcher burgess of Arbroath in 1799. [AA.18.941]

CHAPEL, WILLIAM was admitted as a weaver burgess of Arbroath in 1797. [AA.18.941]

CHAPLINE, Reverend ALEXANDER, in Kinnell, was admitted as a burgess of Arbroath in 1791. [AA.18.941]

CHAPMAN, ANDREW, harpooner aboard the Dorothy of Dundee bound for the Davis Straits in 1825. [NRS.E508.130.8]

CHAPMAN, JAMES, harpooner aboard the Princess Charlotte of Dundee bound for the Davis Strait in 1824. [NRS.E508.129.8]

CHISHOLM, ALEXANDER, was admitted as a wright burgess of Arbroath in 1797. [AA.18.941]

CHRISTISON, HUGH, in Corhairncross, Lochlee, a Precept of Removal, 1815. [NRS.GD45.18.2358]

CHRISTIE, ALEXANDER, a butcher in Arbroath, versus Robert Small and Alexander Lawson, writers in Arbroath, 1815. [NRS.CS42.13.85]

CHRISTIE, GEORGE, was admitted as a merchant burgess of Arbroath in 1795. [AA.18.941]

CHRISTIE, JAMES, was admitted as a burgess of Arbroath in 1799. [AA.18.941]

CHRISTIE, ROBERT, in Wardmill Croft, Arbroath, a victim of theft in 1832. [NRS.AD14.32.130]

CHRISTIE, WILLIAM, was admitted as a mason burgess of Arbroath in 1797. [AA.18.941]

CHRISTIE, Captain, master of the Emma of Dundee from Dundee bound for Quebec in 1848. [EEC]

CHRISTOPHER, ADAM, a skipper at the Fishmarket, Dundee, master of the Estridge of Dundee in 1809. [DD]

CHRISTOPHER, WILLIAM, born 1769, master of the Jane of Dundee in 1809, died 1817, husband of Mary Gall. [DD][Howff gravestone, Dundee]

CLERK, AGNES, daughter of Alexander Clark a shoemaker in Dundee, versus James Balfour, a manufacturer in Dundee, a Process of Divorce, 1803. [NRS.CC8.6.1150]

CLARK, DAVID, master of the Commerce of Dundee trading between St Petersburg and Dundee in 1819. [NRS.E504.11.21]

CLARK, DAVID, a mason in Gravesend, Arbroath, accused of bigamy in 1842. [NRS.AD14.42.36]

CLARK, GEORGE, a skipper on the Shore, Dundee, in 1782, [DD]; master of the Peggy of Dundee in 1797, [NRS.CE70.1.8.64]; in Westhaven of Panbride, testament, 1817. [NRS.CC3]

CLARK, GEORGE, a mason in Panbride, versus Robert Mill, schoolmaster of Monikie, in 1801. [NRS.CS271.180]

CLARK, JAMES, was admitted as a baker burgess of Arbroath in 1794. [AA.8.941]

CLARK, JOHN, was admitted as a merchant burgess of Arbroath in 1794. [AA.8.941]

CLARK, JOHN, a book hawker in City Road, Brechin, was accused of bigamy in 1845. [NRS.AD14.45.153]

CLARK, THOMAS, born 1755, Captain of the $63^{rd}$ Regiment, and of the Forfar and Kincardineshire Militia, died 1842. [Montrose Episcopal gravestone]

CLARK, THOMAS, a burgess of Dundee in 1797, [DBR]; master of the George of Dundee in 1798, [NRS.CE70.1.8]; and of the Betsey Clark and of the George of Dundee in 1809, [DD]; testament 1810, [NRS.CC3]

CLAYSON, EDWARD, of the frigate Champion, was admitted as a burgess of Arbroath in 1790. [AA.8.941]

CLINK, ANN, born 12 May 1833, daughter of Robert Clink and his wife Ann Stuart, married George Small Kiddie in Dundee in 1860, emigrated to Victoria, British Columbia, by 1864, settled in Washington Territory by 1869, died in Seattle, Washngton, on 28 June 1910. [WSP]

CLYNE, WILLIAM, son of James Clyne in Menmuir, a student at Marischal College, Aberdeen, around 1816. [MCA]

COCHRANE, WILLIAM JOHNSON, born on 1 May 1797 in Dundee, son of John Cochrane and his wife Helen Thornton, a tailor who emigrated to America on 1 May 1820, and was naturalised in New York on 27 March 1834. [NARA] [N.Y. Superior Court Records]

COCKBURN, Sir WILLIAM, was admitted as a burgess of Arbroath in 1795. [AA.18.941]

COLLIE, ALEXANDER, born 1783, a labourer who emigrated from Dundee on the barque Herald bound for Charleston, South Carolina, in 1826. [NARA]

COLLENG, Captain SAMUEL, was admitted as a baker burgess of Arbroath in 1797. [AA.18.941]

COLVILLE, JOHN, born 1764, town clerk of Arbroath in 1788, died in 1812, husband of Catherine Mudie. [NRS.CS271.34688][Arbroath Abbey gravestone]

COLVILLE, JOHN BARCLAY, born 1838, son of Andrew Colville and his wife Elisabeth Davidson, a skipper who died in Melbourne, Australia, on 16 December 1897. [Rosehill gravestone, Montrose]

COLVILLE, ROBERT, a weaver in the Roods, Kirriemuir, was accused of theft in 1845. [NRS.AD14.45.228]

CONACHER, JAMES, son of James Conacher in Dundee, was educated at Marischal College, Aberdeen, in 1846, settled in Australia. [MCA]

CONNELL, JAMES, born 1819, a blacksmith in Marketgait, Arbroath, was accused of the murder of John Cromarty a sailor, in 1843. [NRS.AD14.43.373]

CONSTABLE, JAMES, born 1763, son of David Constable, '28 years in Jamaica as a medical practitioner', died on 24 October 1821. [Howff gravestone, Dundee]

CONSTABLE, JAMES, steersman aboard the Dorothy of Dundee bound for the Davis Straits in 1825. [NRS.E508.130.8]

COOK, ANDREW, a farm labourer from Dundee, emigrated to Hobart, Tasmania, Australia, aboard the Marco Polo in 1855. [SRA.TD292]

COOK, JEAN, at the Feus of Tarry, Marywell, St Vigeans, found guilty of child murder, was sentenced to be transported to the colonies for 10 years in 1844. [NRS.JC26.1844.105]

COOK, JOHN, a fresh or green man aboard the Estridge of Dundee, bound for the Davis Straits in 1824. [NRS.E508.129.8]

COOK, WILLIAM, steersman of the Friendship of Dundee at the Davis Straits in 1824. [NRS.E508.130.8]

COOPER, DAVID, born 26 March 1741 in Edzell, died at Montego Bay, Jamaica, on 11 July 179-. [Montego Bay gravestone]

COOPER, DAVID, son of George Cooper a merchant in Slateford, Edzell, died in Jamaica on 4 January 1820. [AJ.3663]

COOPER, JOHN, master of the New Fair Trader of Dundee in 1809. [DD]

COPLAND, JOHN, in Aberdeen, was admitted as a burgess of Arbroath in 1792. [AA.18.941]

COPLAND, JOHN, from Angus, graduated MA from King's College, Aberdeen, in March 1828. [KCA]

CORSAR, JOHN, was admitted as a weaver burgess of Arbroath in 1797. [AA.18.941]

CORSAR, WILLIAM, a land surveyor in Dundee, plan of the estate of Turin, Angus, 1830. [NRS.RHP.3516]

COSSANS, JOHN, was admitted as a brewer burgess of Arbroath in 1797. [AA.18.941]

COSSANS, JOHN, harpooner aboard the Princess Charlotte of Dundee bound for the Davis Strait in 1824. [NRS.E508.129.8]

COULLIE, HELEN, spouse of James Balfour a shoemaker in Maryton, now in Montrose, testament, 1800, Comm. Brechin. [NRS]

COUPAR, ARTHUR, apprentice aboard the Estridge of Dundee, bound for the Davis Strait in 1824. [NRS.E508.129.8]

COUPAR ISABELL WILKIE, wife of John Gunn in High Street, Arbroath, was accused of reset in 1842. [NRS.AD14.42.272]

COUPAR, JOHN, sailor aboard the Estridge of Dundee, bound for the Davis Straits in 1824. [NRS.E508.129.8]

COUTTS, JAMES, born in Arbroath on 2 April 1847, died in San Francisco, California, on 4 June 1911. [San Francisco Bulletin, 5.6.1911]

COWAN, THOMAS, born 1724, a baker, died 1807, husband of Janet Millar, born 1717, died 1792. [Howff gravestone, Dundee]

COWIE, JAMES, born 20 April 1794, died at San Salvador on 5 June 1826. [Montrose gravestone]

COWIE, WILLIAM, born 20 July 1809, died crossing the Mississanga on 28 April 1836, interred at Port Mississanga, Lake Huron. [Montrose gravestone]

COWLET, SAMUEL NORMAN, was admitted as a burgess of Arbroath in 1798. [AA.18.941]

COWLEY, JOHN, a merchant in London, was admitted as a burgess of Arbroath in 1791. [AA.18.941]

CRABB, JOHN, a merchant, imprisoned in Brechin Tolbooth suspected of forgery, found not guilty in 1827. [NRS.JC26.1827.23]

CRABB, WILLIAM, in Montrose, graduated MD from King's College, Aberdeen, on 30 July 1807. [KCA]

CRAICK, DAVID, was admitted as a weaver burgess of Arbroath in 1799. [AA.18.941]

CRAICK, PETER, was admitted as a weaver burgess of Arbroath in 1799. [AA.18.941]

CRAIG, ALEXANDER, master of the Glasgow of Dundee trading between St Petersburg, Russia, and Dundee in 1818. [NRS.E504.11.21]

CRAIG, JEAN, wife of William Morrison a private in the Aberdeenshire Militia, in Montrose, was accused of mobbing and rioting there in 1813. [NRS.AD14.13.84]

CRAIG, PETER, was admitted as a weaver burgess of Arbroath in 1799. [AA.18.941]

CRAIGIE, JOHN, son of Alexander Craigie in Montrose, a student at Marischal College, Aberdeen, graduated MA in 1825. [MCA]

CRAIK, JAMES, a cattle dealer in Aberlemno, 1840. [NRS.CS280.8.5]

CRAIK, JOHN, a porter in Dundee, 1798. [DCA.B19.3.27/4]

CRAIK, MARGARET, a widow, at Northgate, Noranside, Fearn, a victim of housebreaking and theft in 1831. [NRS.A14.31.19]

CRAIK, MARY, daughter of John Craik a tenant of Balglassie, versus her husband James Windrum, tenant in Haughmuir near Brechin, in 1809, a Process of Separation. [NRS.CS8.6.1360]

CRAMOND, JAMES, a messenger in Dundee, testament, 13 May 1795, Comm. Brechin. [NRS]

CRAWFORD, JOHN, steersman of the Friendship of Dundee at the Davis Straits in 1824. [NRS.E508.130.8]

CRAWFORD, JOHN, an apprentice aboard the Dorothy of Dundee bound for the Davis Straits in 1825. [NRS.E508.130.8]

CREE, JAMES, a mariner in Arbroath, and his spouse Jean Mitchell, testament, 1791, Comm, St Andrews. [NRS]

CRIGHTON, DAVID, son of George Crighton a farmer in Finavon, a student at Marischal College, Aberdeen, in 1841. [MCA]

CRICHTON, GEORGE, farmer at Hatton of Newtyle in 1803. [NRS.CS271.528]

CRICHTON, JOHN, surgeon aboard the Friendship of Dundee at the Davis Straits in 1824. [NRS.E508.130.8]

CRIGHTON, ROBERT WILKIE, SON OF George Crighton a farmer in Oathlaw, a student at Marischal College, Aberdeen, in 1843, graduated MD from Edinburgh University in 1849. [MCA]

CRICHTON, THOMAS, born 1712, a merchant and former bailie of Dundee, died 1791, testament, 26 January 1792, Comm. Brechin. [NRS] [Howff gravestone, Dundee]

CRICHTON, WILLIAM, born 1766, a shipmaster in Arbroath, died in 1800, husband of Mary Hackney, born 1761, died in 1837. [Arbroath Abbey gravestone]

CROAL, ALEXANDER, born 1835, died in Demerara in February 1853. [Barry gravestone]

CROAL, ROBERT WEIR, born 1845, died in Shanghai, China, on 5 May 1897. [Barry gravestone]

CROALL, WILLIAM, and his wife Margaret ..., parents of Alexander Croall, born 1850, died in Australia in 1887, and of David Croall, born 1840, died in Australia in 1893. [Farnell gravestone]

CROOKSHANKS, CHARLES, was admitted as a weaver burgess of Arbroath in 1797. [AA.18.947]

CROOKSHANKS, DAVID, a labourer in Lochee, versus Ann Forrest, daughter of John Forrest a miller in Glamis, a Process of Divorce, 1827. [NRS.CC8.6.2065]

CROOM, GEORGE, son of George Croom in Montrose, a student at Marischal College, Aberdeen, in 1826. [MCA]

CROOM, MARY, daughter of George Croom, a merchant in Monifieth, married William Keith, a surgeon of Union Place Aberdeen, in Dundee on 27 December 1825. [SM.97.254]

CROW, JOHN, in the Service of the Honourable East India Company in Bengal, India, later in Dundee, testament, 12 June 1819. [NRS.CC3.3.5.293]

CROW, JOHN, born 2 November 1783 in Dundee, son of Peter Crow and his wife Helen Jack, emigrated to America before 1816, settled in North Carolina in 1819, in Fayetteville, N.C., by 1822, naturalised in Cumberland County, N.C. in December 1824, died there on 30 September 1857. [NCA.CR029.301.16][Cross Creek gravestone, N.C.]

CRUICKSHANK, A. A., born 1845, late of Boston, Massachusetts, died in Inverarity on 4 December 1877. [Fearn gravestone]

CRUICKSHANK, FREDERICK, from Kirriemuir, graduated MA from King's College, Aberdeen, in March 1848. [KCA]

CRUICKSHANK, GEORGE, of the Star Hotel, Montrose, 1839. [NRS.CS233.Seqn.c1.79]

CRUICKSHANK, WILLIAM, late of Jamaica, died in Arbroath on 15 September 1817. [S.1.36]

CUMMING, DAVID, steersman aboard the Estridge of Dundee, bound for the Davis Straits in 1824. [NRS.E508.129.8]

CUMMING, GEORGE, steersman aboard the Estridge of Dundee, bound for the Davis Straits in 1824. [NRS.E508.129.8]

CUMMINGS, JOHN, was admitted as a weaver burgess of Arbroath in 1797. [AA.18.947]

CUNNINGHAM, JOHN ARCHIBALD, born 1843, son of John Cunningham and his wife Margaret Archibald, died in Burwood, Sydney, Australia, on 23 August 1880. [Constitution Road gravestone, Dundee]

CURR, JOHN, from Kirriemuir, graduated MA from King's College, Aberdeen, in March 1850. [KCA]

CURRANCE, DAVID, a white iron-smith in Dundee, 1799. [DCA.B19.3.27/15-8]

CURRIE, JOHN, was admitted as a barber burgess of Arbroath in 1797. [AA.18.947]

CUTHBERT, ALBERT, in Balmachie, a Precept of Removal, 181 5. [NRS.GD45.18.2358]

DAKERS, COLIN, son of David Dakers in Brechin, a student in Marischal College in 1790s., graduated MD from Glasgow University in 1822. [MCA]

DAKERS, WILLIAM, born 1834, son of George Dakers and his wife Isabel Greig, died in Australia on 18 November 1877. [Rosehill gravestone, Montrose]

DALGAIRNS, JAMES, in Balgavies, Aberlemno, was the victim of housebreaking in 1830. [NRS.AD14.30.56; JC26.1830.16]

DALGITY, ALEXANDER, was admitted as a baker burgess of Arbroath in 1796. [AA.18.947]

DALGITY, JOHN, was admitted as a watchmaker burgess of Arbroath in 1797. [AA.18.947]

DALGITY, THOMAS, was admitted as a shoemaker burgess of Arbroath in 1797. [AA.18.947]

DALL, GEORGE, in Dundee, a purser of the Royal Navy, testament, 1814, [NRS.CC3]

DALMAHOY, ROBERT, a merchant and saddler in Brechin, testament, 1795, Comm. Brechin. [NRS]

DANCERS, JOHN, was admitted as a heckler burgess of Arbroath in 1797. [AA.18.947]

DAVIDSON, Reverend DAVID, DD, born 11 February 1750, ordained on 2 January 1776, admitted as a minister of Dundee on 18 July 1782, did there on 22 December 1825. [SM.97.255]

DAVIDSON, DAVID, a shipmaster in Murraygait, Dundee, 1798. [DCA.B19.3.27/14]

DAVIDSON, DAVID, at Brechin Castle, an account, 1818-1819. [NRS.GD45.13.2200]

DAVIDSON, DAVID, a slater in Dundee, died on 14 December 1853, father of David Davidson a slater in Melbourne, Australia. [NRS.S/H.1854]

DAVIDSON, JAMES, an apprentice aboard the Friendship of Dundee at the Davis Straits in 1824. [NRS.E508.130.8]

DAVIDSON, JAMES, son of James Davidson a stonecutter in Montrose, settled in Vancouver, British Columbia, by 1864. [NRS.S/H]

DAVIDSON, JOHN, [1790-1827], and his wife Elizabeth McNicoll, [1794-1820], parents of James Davidson, born 1817, settled in Australia, died on the Orwell on 27 January 1862, and John Davidson, who settled in Victoria, Australia. [Cortachy gravestone]

DAVIDSON, JOHN, of the Brotherly Seaman Society of Montrose, versus …..Young and others of the United Seaman Society of Montrose, in 1841. [NRS.CS237.D11.14]

DAVIDSON, WILLIAM, Captain of Lord Lindsay's Regiment of Foot, was admitted as a burgess of Arbroath in 1797. [AA.18.967]

DAVIDSON, ……, master of the Thomas in 1836. [HS.18.1.19]

DAVIDSON, ROBERT, mate and harpooner aboard the Estridge of Dundee bound for the Davis Straits in 1824. [NRS.E508.129.8]

DAVIDSON, THOMAS, a farm servant to David Davidson farmer at the Mains of Guynd, Carmyllie, was accused of assault in 1845. [NRS.AD14.45.230]

DAVIE, DONALD, a labourer in Charleston, Glamis, was accused of theft in 1839. [NRS.AD14.39.130]

DAWSON, WILLIAM, an apprentice boot and shoemaker in Montrose, was accused of mobbing and rioting there in 1813. [NRS.AD14.13.84]

DEACON, JAMES, born 1744, a Captain of the Royal Navy, died in 1813. [Montrose gravestone]

DEADRICK, JOHN, sailor aboard the Estridge of Dundee bound for the Davis Straits in 1824. [NRS.E508.129.8]

DEAR, DAVID, was admitted as a weaver burgess of Arbroath in 1796. [AA.18.947]

DEMPSTER, ALEXANDER, a flax dresser in Nether Tenements of Caldhame near Brechin, 1850. [NRS.E859.83]

DEMPSTER, GEORGE, of Dunnichen, versus Reverend James Headrick in Dunnichen in 1812. [NRS.CS271.62538]

DEMPSTER, THOMAS, born 1810, son of Thomas Dempster and his wife Euphemia McKay, died in Melbourne, Australia, in 1884. [Constitution Road gravestone, Dundee]

DEUCHARS, ALEXANDER, master of the Intrepid, 1860. [HS.18.1.17]

DEUCHARS, GEORGE, a skipper in Seagait, Dundee, 1818, [DD]; master of the Estridge of Dundee bound for the Davis Straits in 1824, [NRS.E508.129.8]; in 1825, [DSR]; testament, 1845. [NRS.SC45.31.7.127]

DEUCHARS, JAMES, mate and harpooner of the Dorothy of Dundee bound for the Davis Straits in 1825. [NRS.E508.130.8]

DEUCHARS, WILLIAM, master of the Mary Ann of Dundee from 1803-1811. [HS.18.1.17][NRS.E508]; master of the Dorothy in 1824. [DD]

DEUCHARS, ....., master of the Princess Charlotte in 1853. [DD]

DEUCHARS, WILLIAM, born 1771, a skipper in Seagait, Dundee, 1809, [DD], master of the William and Jean of Dundee in 1798, [NRS.CE70.1.8/31]; master of the Mary Ann of Dundee in 1813-1818, [NRS.E508.115.8]; died 1824. [Howff gravestone, Dundee]

DICK, DAVID, born 1709, weaver in Broughty Ferry, died 17 August 1797, husband of Ann Ramsay, born 1730, died 21 April 1818. [Murroes gravestone]

DICK, DAVID, born 1829, son of Andrew Dick and his wife Elizabeth Dalgetty, died 31 March 1870, buried in Greymouth, Westland, New Zealand. [Dunnichen gravestone]

DICK, JAMES, born 1720, a merchant and Cess-collector in Dundee, died 1808, husband of Christina Wardroper, born 1728, died 1793. [Howff gravestone, Dundee]

DICK, THOMAS, born 1739, died 1787, husband of Ann Nairn, born 1731, died 1816. [Howff gravestone, Dundee]

DICK, WILLIAM, [1765-1816], a machine maker in Dundee, and his wife Euphemia Drummond, [1771-1835], parents of Robert Dick, born 1806, a merchant in Trinidad, died at sea off Grenada on 24 July 1845, also of William Dick, born 1799, died in Montgomery, Alabama, in January 1832. [Dundee gravestone]

DICKSON, DAVID, at Northgate, Noranside, Fearn, a victim of housebreaking and theft in 1831. [NRS.A14.31.19]

DICKSON, JOHN, master of the Anna of Dundee in 1809. [DD]

DICKSON, WILLIAM, died in 1798, husband of Christian Gordon who died in 1807. [Montrose, Episcopal, gravestone]

DICKSON, WILLIAM, a stationer from Dundee, married Elizabeth Leighton Bowie, daughter of William Bowie in New York, in Edinburgh on 20 June 1842. [SG.11.1199]

DIDRICK, COLIN, line manager of the Friendship of Dundee at the Davis Straits in 1824. [NRS.E508.130.8]

DOIG, Mrs ELIZABETH, spouse of David Doig a weaver in Dryburgh Green, testament, 20 June 1797, Comm. Brechin. [NRS]

DOIG, JAMES, in Antigua, heir to his cousin Ann Doig or Riddell of Cookston in 1791, [NRS.S/H]; in St John, Antigua, disposed of the lands of Cookston, Brechin, to Walter Riddell in 1792. [NRS.RD2.255.122]

DOIG, JAMES, a merchant in Dundee, invoices, 1796-1809. [NRS.CS96.1605]

DOIG, JAMES, a manufacturer in Dundee, father of Thomas Doig who died in Pescadera, Santa Cruz County, California, on 27 November 1863. [EFR]

DOIG, Reverend JOHN, was admitted as a burgess of Arbroath in 1791. [AA.18.947]

DOIG, JOHN, son of John Doig a farmer in Tannadice, a student at Marischal College, Aberdeen, around 1818. [MCA]

DOIG, ROBERT, born 1736, a manufacturer in Dundee, died 1802, husband of Margaret Cock who died in 1778. [Howff gravestone, Dundee]

DON, JAMES, son of Alexander Don a farmer in Angus, was educated at Marischal College, Aberdeen, in 1845, later a minister at Kyneston, Victoria, Australia. [MCA]

DON, JOHN DAVIDSON, son of John Don a merchant in Brechin, a student at Marischal College, Aberdeen, in 1840s, later Free Church minister in Calcutta, India, and in South Africa. ;MCA]

DONALD, Mrs ANN, died in New Orleans, Louisiana, on 1 May 1858. [Howff gravestone, Dundee]

DONALD, JAMES, a sailor aboard the Dorothy of Dundee bound for the Davis Straits in 1825. [NRS.E508.130.8]

DONALD, JOHN, son of James Donald in Kirriemuir, died at Montego Bay, Jamaica on 19 May 1819, testament, 1819. Comm. Edinburgh. [NRS]

DONALD, JOHN, a sailor aboard the Dorothy of Dundee bound for the Davis Straits in 1825. [NRS.E508.130.8]

DONALD, WILLIAM, son of Alexander Donald a farmer in Logie Pert, a student at Marischal College, Aberdeen, graduated MA in 1832. [MCA]

DONALDSON, GEORGE, a manufacturer in Carnoustie, a tack, 1840. [NRS.GD45.16]

DONALDSON, JAMES, born 1801, son of William Donaldson and his wife Elizabeth Hill, died in Sydney, Australia, on 17 March 1857. [Old Mains gravestone, Dundee]

DONALDSON, JAMES, master of the Isabella of Dundee from Dundee to Quebec and Montreal in 1830, and 1833. [QM][DPCA.12.1833]

DONNAR, JOHN, a journeyman shoemaker in Overgait, Dundee, was accused of membership of an unlawful combination in 1820. [NRS.AD14.20.215]

DORRAT, JOHNSTON, sailor aboard the Princess Charlotte of Dundee bound for the Davis Strait in 1824. [NRS.E508.129.8]

DORWARD, ROBERT, a shoemaker in Blackscroft, Dundee, in 1799. [DCA.B19.3.27/268]

DOUGAL, THOMAS, a banker in Montrose, father of Margaret Addison Dougal, who married Captain George Bell, in Montrose on 19 June 1820. [SM.86.94]

DOUGAL, THOMAS, a banker in Montrose, father of John Dougal born on 23 August 1807, a merchant in Calcutta, India, died there on 11 April 1834. [NRS.S/H.1830] [South Park gravestone, Calcutta]

DOUGLAS, ALEXANDER, an apprentice aboard the Dorothy of Dundee bound for the Davis Straits in 1825. [NRS.E508.130.8]

DOUGLAS, ANDREW, in Ferryden by Montrose, 1848. [NRS.CS279.653]

DOUGLAS, ARCHIBALD, son of William Douglas a gentleman in Brigton, a student at Marischal College in 1807. [MCA]

DOUGLAS, Mrs CATHERINE, relict of John Douglas a planter in Charleston, South Carolina, testament, 6 September 1816, Brechin. [NRS.CC3.3.14/307]

DOVE, JAMES, from Brechin, graduated MA from King's College, Aberdeen, in March 1842. [KCA]

DOW, ARTHUR, master of the Entmion of Dundee trading between St Petersburg, Russia, and Dundee in 1818. [NRS.E504.11.21]

DOW, Captain, master of the Hunter of Dundee was shored at Narva, Russia, in 1843. [MD.157]

DRUMMOND, JAMES, a shipmaster in Dundee, testament, 31 December 1798, and 11 January 1799, Comm. Brechin. [NRS]

DUFF, ANN, born 1804, daughter of Peter Duff and his wife Ann Keill, died in Christchurch, New Zealand, on 1 November 1834. [Rosehill gravestone, Montrose]

DUFF, ANTHONY D., born 1781 in Dundee, son of Robert Duff, emigrated to New York in 1806, a wine merchant there, died on 20 February 1825. [ANY]

DUFFUS, WILLIAM, master of the Neptune of Dundee trading between Newcastle-on-Tyne and Dundee in 1819. [NRS.E504.11.21]

DUKE, WILLIAM, from Brechin, graduated MA from King's College, Aberdeen, on 1 January 1851, later minister at St Vigeans from 1859 until 1911. [KCA][St Vigeans gravestone]

DUMBRANK, WILLIAM, was admitted as a weaver burgess of Arbroath in 1798. [AA.18.941]

DUN, WILLIAM, a merchant in Forfar, was admitted as a burgess of Arbroath in 1789. [AA.18.941]

DUNCAN, ALEXANDER, a shipmaster in Arbroath, testament, 1803, Comm. St Andrews. [NRS]

DUNCAN, ALEXANDER, born on 26 May 1805 in Arbroath, son of Alexander Duncan of Parkhill, Arbroath, emigrated via Liverpool to New York aboard the Amity, was educated at Yale and Brown Universities, a lawyer in Canandaigua and in Rhode Island, naturalised in N.Y. on 2 March 1827, moved to England in 1863, died in London on 14 October 1889. [ANY.2.298][Craig Inchbrioch gravestone, Montrose][NY Marine Court Records] [NRS.SC70.1.283]

DUNCAN, ANDREW, was admitted as a shipmaster burgess of Arbroath in 1796. [AA.18.941]

DUNCAN, CHARLES ERSKINE, son of Charles Duncan and grandson of Alexander Duncan of Ardownie, a merchant in New York by 1795, [NRS.RD3.271.95; RD3.285.190; CS17.1.4.299]; in New York in 1817. [NRS.CS17.36.618]

DUNCAN, DAVID, born in Arbroath, emigrated via Liverpool to New York aboard the Amity on 14 January 1819, a merchant in New York, died in March 1842. [ANY.2.105]

DUNCAN, DAVID, surgeon of the Princess Charlotte of Dundee bound for the Davis Strait in 1824. [NRS.E508.129.8]

DUNCAN, DAVID, born 1847, son of David Duncan, died in Sydney, Australia, on 9 March 1870. [St Aidan's gravestone, Broughty Ferry]

DUNCAN, DAVID, a jeweller from Montrose, died in New York on 28 September 1877. [S.10,688]

DUNCAN, GEORGE, born 1770 in Dundee, a mariner who was naturalised in Charleston, South Carolina, on 17 June 1799. [NARA.M1183.1]

DUNCAN, JAMES, born 1768, a mason in Montrose, died in 1828. [Montrose gravestone]

DUNCAN, JAMES, was admitted as a wright burgess of Arbroath in 1797. [AA.18.941]

DUNCAN, JAMES, born 1813, son of John Duncan and his wife Margaret Ferrier in Strathcathro, died in Jamaica in 1854. [Brechin gravestone]

DUNCAN, JAMES, a grain and linen merchant in Dundee in 1819. [NRS.CS96.1820]

DUNCAN, JOHN, a preacher and a Chartist in Lyon's Close, Hawkhill, Dundee, was accused of mobbing and rioting in the New Hall, Bell Street, Dundee, in 1842. [NRS.AD14.42.354; JC26.1843.443]

DUNCAN, ROBERT, was admitted as a tailor burgess of Arbroath in 1797. [AA.18.941]

DUNCAN, ROBERT, a fresh or green man aboard the Friendship of Dundee at the Davis Straits in 1824. [NRS.E508.130.8]

DUNCAN, Lord, of Lundie, letters, 1808. [NRS.GD137.3635]

DUNCAN, SUSAN, daughter of Alexander Duncan in Essie, versus her husband Alexander Watt a butcher in Arbroath, a Process of Separation, 1808. [NRS.CC8.6.1306]

DUNCAN, WILLIAM, born 1798, a merchant who emigrated from Dundee on the brig Traveller of Aberdeen bound for Charleston, South Carolina, in 1822. [NARA]

DUNCAN, WILLIAM, son of William Duncan an engineer in Dundee, a student at Marischal College in 1851. [MCA]

DUNCAN, Captain, master of the Duke of Wellington of Dundee was shipwrecked in the Gulf of Finland in 1843. [MD.157]

DUNDAS, DAVID, a mason, was granted a tack in Edzell, in 1843. [NRS.GD45.16.1931]

DUNDAS, ELIZABETH, born 1817, died in Boston, Masachusetts, on 12 March 1882. [Edzell gravestone]

DUNDAS, JAMES, born 1842, settled in Boston, Massachusetts, died in New York on 16 January 1890. [Edzell gravestone]

DUNDAS, WILLIAM, born 1816, died in Boston, Massachusetts, on 12 March 1892. [Edzell gravestone]

DUTCH, WILLIAM, line manager aboard the Dorothy of Dundee, bound for the Davis Straits in 1825. [NRS.E508.130.8]

DYCE, ISABELLA, wife of William Dyce in Spittle Burn, Kinnettles, a victim of a mob and rioters in the New Hall, Bell Street, Dundee, in 1842. [NRS.AD14.42.354; JC26.1843.443]

EASTON, JAMES, a wright at Slateford, Edzell, testament, 24 January 1798, Comm. St Andrews. [NRS]

EASTON, JOHN, MD, a surgeon at Kingston Royal Hospital, eldest son of Reverend Dr Easton in Kirriemuir, died in Kingston, Jamaica, on 13 August 1841. [AJ.4886]

EASTON, ROBERT, in Hodgeton, Inverkeillor, testament, 13 April 1791. Comm. St Andrews. [NRS]

EDGAR, ELIZABETH, wife of Thomas Webster a merchant and Provost of Montrose, testament, 30 July 1792, Comm. Brechin. [NRS]

EDWARDS, JAMES K., from Dundee, graduated MA from King's College, Aberdeen, in March 1847, later in Montreal. [KCA]

ELDER, ALEXANDER, harpooner aboard the Princess Charlotte of Dundee bound for the Davis Strait in 1824. [NRS.E508.129.8]

ELDER, JOHN, master of the Fame of Dundee trading between Riga, Latvia, and Dundee in 1797, and of the Industry bound from Dundee to Riga, Latvia, in 1804. [NRS.CE70.1.8/50][ MF.87]

ELLAS, JOHN, born 1804, son of Alexander Ellas a farmer in West Mains of Gardyne, Kirkden, was accused of assaulting John Sutherland, a messenger at arms, in Forfar, in 1825. [NRS.AD14.25.83]

ELLIOT, THOMAS, master of the Riga Merchant of Dundee, trading between Dundee and Archangel, Russia, in 1803-1804. [NRS.CE70.1.10]

ENSLIE, JOHN, a merchant in Rotterdam, Zealand, was admitted as a burgess of Arbroath in 1791. [AA.18.941]

ERSKINE, ALEXANDER, attorney to John Erskine of Dun, trustee of Lima Estate, Jamaica, records, 1800-1806. [NRS.GD123.454]

ERSKINE, ANN, daughter of Alexander Erskine a merchant in Montrose, testament, 1797, Comm. Brechin. [NRS]

ERSKINE, ALICE, of Dun, versus Reverend Alexander Carnegie, in 1823. [NRS.CS44.34.66]

ERSKINE, GEORGE, tenant in Westside, Edzell, testament, 15 February 1793, Comm. Brechin. [NRS]

ERSKINE, JEAN, daughter of Alexander Erskine a merchant in Montrose, testament, 1797, Comm. Brechin. [NRS]

ERSKINE, JOHN, of Dun, papers, 1810. [NRS.GD123.430]

ERSKINE, N. H. K., of Dun, a petition, 1850. [NRS.CS46.1850.17]

ERSKINE, T., master of the Psyche trading between Dundee, Quebec and Montreal in 1820. [NRS.E504.11.21]

ESPLIN, ALEXANDER, a manufacturer, was admitted as a burgess of Arbroath in 1796. [AA.18.941]

ESSON, DAVID, born 1823, son of George Esson and his wife Janet Stephen, died in Australia on 31 May 1854. [Monikie gravestone]

ESTON, DAVID, a weaver, was admitted as a burgess of Arbroath in 1797. [AA.18.941]

ESTON, JOHN, was admitted as a burgess of Arbroath in 1793. [AA.18.941]

EWAN, ISOBEL, wife of Robert Hutcheon a carter in Montrose, was accused of mobbing and rioting there in 1813. [NRS.AD14.13.84]

EWART, LOUISA, wife of Alexander Smith a flax-dresser in High Street, Arbroath, was accused of reset in 1842. [NRS.AD14.42.272]

EWING, THOMAS, born 1803, son of Peter Ewing in Arbroath, died in Kingston, Jamaica, in 1832. [Arbroath Abbey gravestone]

EYLES, JOHN, born 1773, a surgeon, died in Arbroath on 6 June 1820. [SM.86.190]

FAICHNEY, PATRICK, in Millshades, later in Hawkhill, Dundee, testament, 9 August 1797, Comm. Brechin. [NRS]

FAIRWEATHER, MARY, born 1812, at Law of Craigo, Logie Pert, was accused of deserting a child in 1850. [NRS.AD14.50.187]

FAIRWEATHER, ROBERT, from Brechin, graduated MA from King's College, Aberdeen, in March 1835. [KCA]

FAIRWEATHER, WILLIAM, a blacksmith in Fairlaw Bank, Kirriemuir, and his wife Ann Young, were accused of imprisoning and confining a person of weak intellect and neglect in 1842. [NRS.AD14.42.8]

FALCONER, ROBERT, a merchant, was granted a tack in Slateford, Edzell, in 1838. [NRS.GD45.16.1918]

FARMER, JAMES, master of the Alexander of Dundee, from Archangel, Russia, to Dundee in October 1818, from Dundee bound for New Orleans, Louisiana, in December 1818. [NRS.E504.11.21]

FARQUHAR, JOHN, of Pitscandly, married Mary Ann Shillito, daughter of George Shillito of Upper Thames Street, London, on 17 July 1820. [SM.86.189]

FARQUHARSON, ALEXANDER, fifth son of Innes Farquharson, a cabinet-maker, born in Glamis, and his wife Isabel, daughter of Peter Waller a porter in Dundee, was born on 24 September 1814, and baptised in the Qualified Episcopal Chapel in Dundee on 2 October 1814. [DE.25]

FARQUHARSON, PETER, Quartermaster of the 88th Regiment of Foot, testament, 15 August 1792, Comm. Brechin. [NRS]

FAWNS, ALEXANDER, a labourer in High Street, Brechin, was accused of mobbing and rioting in the High Street of Brechin in 1830. [NRS.AD14.30.89]

FENTON, GEORGE, a labourer in Pyot's Close, Forfar, a victim of theft in 1825. [NRS.AD14.25.244]

FENTON, JOHN, born 1741, a dyer in Dundee, died 1827, husband of Elisabeth Adamson, born 1763, died in 1835. [Howff gravestone, Dundee]

FENTON, PETER, from Angus, graduated MA from King's College, Aberdeen, on 27 March 1795. [KCA]

FENTON, WILLIAM, a journeyman shoemaker in Kirk Wynd, Dundee, was accused of membership of an unlawful combination in 1820. [NRS.AD14.20.215]

FERGUSON, DAVID, son of Reverend Andrew Ferguson in Maryton, a student at Marischal College, Aberdeen, in 1820s, later a Free Church minister in Strachan. [MCA]

FERGUSON, JAMES, a weaver, was granted a tack in Edzell, in 1843. [NRS.GD45.16.1933]

FERGUSON, JEAN, in Dundee, testament, 12 June 1794, Comm. Brechin. [NRS]

FERGUSON, SAMUEL, master of the William and Nancy of Dundee trading between Riga, Latvia, and Dundee in 1818. [NRS.E504.11.21]

FERRIER, ALEXANDER, born 1826, son of Walter Ferrier and his wife Jean McGill, died in Australia on 12 November 1868. [Brechin Cathedral gravestone]

FERRIER, CATHERINE, born 1829, daughter of Walter Ferrier and his wife Jean McGill, wife of Dr Richter, died in Lyndoch Valley, South Australia on 3 May 1902. [Brechin Cathedral gravestone]

FERRIER, CHARLES, a weaver, was admitted as a burgess of Arbroath in 1797. [AA.18.941]

FERRIER, GEORGE, born 1833, son of Walter Ferrier and his wife Jean McGill, died in Riverton, South Australia on 21 June 1906. [Brechin Cathedral gravestone]

FERRIER, JOHN, master of the Betsey of Dundee in 1809. [DD]

FERRIER, SAMUEL, a weaver, was admitted as a burgess of Arbroath in 1799. [AA.18.941]

FIFE, DAVID, a merchant, was admitted as a burgess of Arbroath in 1791. [AA.18.941]

FINDALE, JAMES, a shoemaker in Forfar, testament, 1796, Comm. St Andrews. [NRS]

FINDLAY, FRANCIS, in Middleshade, Brechin, testament, 13 July 1798, Comm. Brechin. [NRS]

FINDLAY, JAMES, sailor aboard the Estridge of Dundee, bound for the Davis Straits in 1824. [NRS.E508.129.8]

FINLAY, ALEXANDER, born 1750, a shipmaster in Dundee, died in 1826, husband of Margaret Kidd, born 1753, died 1834. [Howff gravestone, Dundee]

FINLAY, CHARLES, in Broughty Ferry, versus James Soutar a merchant in Dundee in 1821. [NRS.CS44.189.50]

FINLAY, DAVID, harpooner of the Friendship of Dundee at the Davis Straits in 1824. [NRS.E508.130.8]

FINDLAY, PATRICK, a merchant, was admitted as a burgess of Arbroath in 1797. [AA.18.941]

FINDLAY, ROBERT, a weaver, was admitted as a burgess of Arbroath in 1797. [AA.18.941]

FINDLAY, WILLIAM, son of David Finlay in Brechin, graduated MA from Marischal College in 1808, later a schoolmaster in Fraserburgh, then a minister in King Edward, Aberdeenshire. [MCA]

FINLAYSON, JAMES, a farmer in Friockheim, father of James Finlayson a millwright in Payson, Utah, by 1871. [NRS.S/H]

FITCHET, ALEXANDER, born 1792, son of John Fitchet a merchant in Montrose, died in Jamaica on 20 February 1822.

FITCHET, ALEXANDER, born 1823, died at Gighty Burn on 16 August 1904, husband of Ann Salmond, born 1824, died at Cotton of Letham on 24 February 1878. [St Vigeans gravestone]

FITCHET, ALEXANDER, in Muirdrum, a tack, 1840. [NRS.GD45.16]

FITCHET, JOHN, a tailor from Grangepans, was admitted as a burgess of Arbroath in 1791. [AA.18.941]

FITCHET, JOHN, in Muirdrum, a letter, 1803. [NRS.GD45.14.537]

FITCHET, WILLIAM, born 1716, a merchant and bailie of Arbroath, died 1796, testament, 1800, Comm. St Andrews. [NRS]

FITCHIE, BARBARA, in Monikie, a tack, 1840. [NRS.GD45.16]

FLEMING, JOHN, in Arbroath, exported a cargo of linen via Dundee aboard the Comely, Captain Gray, bound for Charleston, South Carolina, in August 1820. [NRS.E504.11.21]

FLETCHER, ANN, widow of Alexander Read of Logie, a trust disposition, 1806. [NRS.GD1.196.7]

FLUCKHART, WILLIAM, master of the Helen of Montrose from Montrose to Quebec in 1855, 1856. [AJ][QM]

FORBES, JAMES, a merchant, was admitted as a burgess of Arbroath in 1791. [AA.18.941]

FORBES, JOHN, a carpenter in Dundee, was accused of assault in 1819. [NRS.AD14.19.167]

FORBES, MARGART, in Balmachie, a tack, 1840. [NRS.GD45.16]

FORBES, PETER, born 1741, died in 1796. [Howff gravestone, Dundee]

FORDYCE, GEORGE, a quarrier in Leysmill, accused of horse stealing in 1844. [NRS.AD14.44.25]

FORDYCE, ......, in London, was admitted as a burgess of Arbroath in 1791. [AA.18.941]

FOREMAN, DAVID, line manager of the Friendship of Dundee at the Davis Straits in 1824. [NRS.E508.130.8]

FOREMAN, JOHN, a shipmaster in Dundee, son of David Foreman a shipmaster burgess, was admitted as a burgess of Dundee on 3 September 1828. [DBR]

FOREMAN, ROBERT, master of the Three Brothers, in 1824. [DD]

FORSYTH, JAMES, born 1842, died in Rydalmere, Australia, on 7 May 1917. [Forfar gravestone]

FOSTER, JOSEPH, was murdered at Guildy Muir, Monikie, in 1847. [NRS.AD14.47.120]

FOTHERINGHAM, HELEN, daughter of Dr David Fotheringham in Dundee, testament, 17 October 1792, Comm. Brechin. [NRS]

FOWLER, PETER, a shoemaker in Arbirlot, a tack, 1840. [NRS.GD45.16.1732]

FOY, JOHN, born 1790, a labourer at Pitairlie Quarry, died in September 1850. [Monifieth burial]

FOX, BRUCE, a weaver in Carnoustie, a tack, 1840. [NRS.GD45.16]

FOX, JOHN, born 1841, son of Bruce Fox and his wife Margaret Kidd, died in Sydney, Australia, on 30 May 1890. [Panbride gravestone]

FRASER, ALEXANDER, born 1760 in Montrose, a mariner who was naturalised in South Carolina in 1792. [NARA.M1183.1]

FRASER, ALEXANDER, in Farmtoun of Lydiat, Lundie, a victim of theft in 1835. [NRS.AD14.35.141.2]

FRASER, JAMES, born 1829, died in Allitown, Australia, on 4 September 1878. [Forfar gravestone]

FRASER, JOHN, was admitted as a burgess of Arbroath in 1794. [AA.18.941]

FROGGATT, CORNELIUS, master of the brigantine Rodney, 1790-1805, husband of Jean Thomson. [Howff gravestone, Dundee] [HS.18.1.20]

FULLERTON, JAMES STRACHAN, born 13 June 1757 at Mains of Dun, son of George Fullerton, [1714-1774], a Halifax, Nova Scotia, in 1780s, later a farmer, died 8 May 1852 at the Halifax River, N.S. [FNA]

FYALL, JAMES, steersman of the Friendship of Dundee at the Davis Straits in 1824. [NRS.E508.130.8]

FYFFE, CHARLES, youngest son of David Fyffe of Drumgeith, died in Jamaica on 15 October 1801. [CM.121847][GM.74.86][.77]DPCA.77]

FYFFE, DAVID, in Dundee, late in Jamaica, a sasine, 1781. [NRS.Forfar.39]

FYFFE, JAMES, sr. and jr, in Chapelton, Kirriemuir, a victim of forgery in 1832. [NRS.AD14.32.27]

FYFFE, JAMES ECKFORD, son of David Fyffe in Monikie, a student at Marischal College in the 1840s, later minister of the United Presbyterian Church in Kilmacolm. [MCA]

FYFFE, JOHN, born 1742, a skipper in Dundee, died in 1821, [Howff gravestone]; testament, 1822, [NRS]

FYFE, JOHN, from Carmylie, graduated MA from King's College, Aberdeen, in March 1848, later a librarian and Professor of Moral Philosophy. [KCA]

FYFE, WILLIAM, from Kirriemuir, graduated MA from King's College, Aberdeen, in March 1841. [KCA]

GALL, JAMES, master of the Arrow of Dundee in 1809. [DD]

GALLOWAY, DAVID, a merchant in Dundee, 1798. [DCA.B19.3.27/1]

GALLOWAY, JANET, in Dundee, testament, 10 June 1794, Comm. Brechin. [NRS]

GALLOWAY, JESSIE, in Andover, Massachusetts, by 1851, daughter of William Galloway a baker in Brechin. [NRS.S/H.1951]

GALLOWAY, JOHN, a flax-dresser in Chapelshade, Dundee, 1796, husband of Margaret Duncan, born 1722, died 1795. [Howff gravestone, Dundee]

GALLOWAY, JOHN, born 1812, son of John Galloway and his wife Ann Lamb, died in New York on 30 November 1840. [Arbroath Abbey gravestone]

GARDINER, JAMES, a tinsmith from Dundee, with his wife and family, settled in Salt Lake City, Utah, and by 1863 in Minneapolis, Minnesota. [DCA.GD.X58]

GARDINER, JOHN, from Dundee, settled in Virginia, probate in November 1816, PCC. [TNA]

GARDNER, DAVID, of Kirktonhill, born 1723, a merchant in Montrose, died 1794, husband of Elizabeth Coutts, born 1741, died 1825 testament, 1797, Comm. Brechin. [NRS]; [Montrose, Episcopal gravestone]

GARDYNE, JAMES, of Middleton, parish of Arbroath, testament, 1790, Comm. St Andrews. [NRS]

GARDYNE, JAMES, in Milton of Carmyllie, a victim of housebreakers in 1830. [NRS.AD14.30.90; JC26.1830.17]

GARDYNE, JAMES WILLIAM, son of William B. Gardyne of Middleton, a student at Marischal College, Aberdeen, in 1840s, later minister of the Scots Kirk in Demerara. [MCA]

GARDYNE, THOMAS, of Middleton, born 1780, died 1840, papers. [NRS.NRAS 022]

GEIKIE, HENRY, a merchant and former Provost of Dundee, testament,1792, Comm. Brechin. [NRS]

GEIKIE, JAMES HENRY, from Arbroath, settled on Colonel's Island, Glynn County, Georgia, married Catherine Amelia Gamble, father of

Catherine Caroline Eleanora Geikie, born 11 August 1807, baptised on 24 March 1811. [Arbroath Old Parish Register]

GEEKIE, ROBERT, of Brown Street, Dundee, an officer of the law, was assaulted in Trottick in 1837. [NRS.AD14.37.123]

GEEKIE, WILLIAM, from Arbroath, a sailor in the Royal Navy before 1763, settled at Goose Creek, South Carolina, as a planter, a Loyalist in 1776, returned to Arbroath by 1784, a merchant there, testament, 1793, Comm. St Andrews. [NRS][TNA.AO.12.50.138, etc][NRS.CS97.103.7]

GELLATLEY, JAMES, an apprentice aboard the Friendship of Dundee at the Davis Straits in 1824. [NRS.E508.130.8]

GELLATLY, JOHN, son of John Gellatly, died 1839, and his wife Elizabeth Smith, died 1840, a banker in Geelong, Australia, by 1855. [Constitution Road gravestone, Dundee]

GIBB, ANDREW, a carter and vintner in High Street, Forfar, , was accused of housebreaking at Balgavies, Aberlemno, in 1830. [NRS.AD14.30.56; JC26.1830.16]

GIBB, DANIEL, born 1746, a ships carpenter, died in 1816, husband of Janet Myers, born 1749, died 1822. [Montrose gravestone]

GIBB, DAVID, born 1833, son of Alexander Gibb and his wife Margaret Addison, died in Australia on 8 May 1857, [Western gravestone, Dundee]

GIB, WILLIAM, Customs Surveyor at Montrose, was admitted as a burgess of Arbroath in 1796. [AA.18.941]

GIBSON, DAVID, an apprentice aboard the Princess Charlotte of Dundee bound for the Davis Strait in 1824. [NRS.E508.129.8]

GIBSON, JAMES, from Angus, graduated MA from King's College, Aberdeen, on 30 March 1790. [KCA]

GIBSON, JOHN, was admitted as a burgess of Dundee in 1771, [DBR]; master of the Duke of Cumberland of Dundee in 1795, and the Janet and Graham of Dundee in 1798, [NRS.CE70.1.8/47; 58]; a resident of Tindall's Wynd, Dundee, in 1809. [DD]

GIBSON, PATRICK, a weaver, was admitted as a burgess of Arbroath in 1795. [AA.18.941]

GIBSON, WILLIAM, son of George Gibson in Arbroath, a student at Marischal College, Aberdeen in 1820s. [MCA]

GILBERT, THOMAS, a journeyman shoemaker in Bucklemaker Wynd, Dundee, was accused of membership of an unlawful combination in 1820. [NRS.AD14.20.215]

GILCHRIST, JOHN, steersman aboard the Estridge of Dundee, bound for the Davis Straits in 1824. [NRS.E508.129.8]

GILLIES, COLIN, a merchant in Brechin, sederunt books, 1818-1825. [NRS.CS96.3620]

GILLIES, ROBERT, from Angus, graduated MA from King's College, Aberdeen, in March 1825. [KCA]

GILLIEVRAY, ARCHIBALD, a merchant, was admitted as a burgess of Arbroath in 1797. [AA.18.941]

GILROY, JOHN, a sailor aboard the Friendship of Dundee at the Davis Straits in 1824. 1757[NRS.E508.130.8]

GLEGG, ADAM, in Montrose, in 1779, a merchant and former Provost of Montrose, died in London in 1807, husband of Ann Smith, born 1738, died 1811. [Montrose gravestone] [NRS.E326.3.19]

GLEGG, JAMES, born 1764, a surgeon in the Royal Navy, died in 1807. [Montrose, Episcopal gravestone]

GLEGG, ROBERT, a Customs land-waiter in Montrose, testament, 1791, Comm. Brechin. [NRS]

GLEIG, Reverend GEORGE, born in Brechin, son of George Gleig a blacksmith, graduated MA in Aberdeen in 1777, minister of Arbroath from 1788 until 1835, husband of Mary Duncan. [F.5.425]

GOLD, ALEXANDER, tenant in Ardgeith, parishes of Lethnot and Navar, testament, 1793, Comm. Brechin. [NRS]

GOLD, ALEXANDER, a flax dresser, was admitted as a burgess of Arbroath in 1797. [AA.18.941]

GOLLENS, COLIN, from Dundee, father of Ann How Gollens who married David Henderson from Perth, in St Louis, Missouri, in 1872. [S.9073]

GOODALE, JAMES, a merchant, was admitted as a burgess of Arbroath in 1799. [AA.18.941]

GOODLET, JEAN, daughter of ...Goodlet a weaver in Dundee, versus William Forrester, a labourer at the Whim, a Process of Adherence, 1810. [NRS.CC8.6.410]

GORDON, ALEXANDER, from Montrose, a theological student in 1812, emigrated to America. [UPC]

GORDON, ANDREW, was admitted as a burgess of Arbroath in 1797. [AA.18.941]

GORDON, ANDREW, a sailor aboard the Friendship of Dundee at the Davis Straits in 1824. [NRS.E508.130.8]

GORDON, CHARLES, minister of Cortachy and Clova, testament, 1795, Comm. Brechin. [NRS]

GORDON, DAVID, Captain of the 134$^{th}$ Regiment, was admitted as a burgess of Arbroath in 1795. [AA.18.941]

GORDON, EDWARD, born 1844 son of George Gordon of Riga and Montrose, died at sea on 6 May 1885. [S.13068]

GORDON, GEORGE, from Arbroath, graduated MA from King's College, Aberdeen, in March 1858, later a school master in Manchester. [KCA]

GORDON, ISABEL, second daughter of William Gordon in Montrose, married Edward Dickson from New York, in Montrose on 16 May 1843. [AJ.4973]

GORDON, JAMES, son of James Gordon in Kirriemuir, a student in Marischal College, Aberdeen, in 1790s [MCA]

GORDON, JAMES, son of William Gordon in Dundee, a student in Marischal College, Aberdeen, in 1790s. [MCA]

GORDON, JAMES, from Angus, graduated MA from King's College, Aberdeen, on 29 March 1802. [KCA]

GORDON, JAMES, son of William Gordon in Dundee, graduated MA from Marischal College, Aberdeen, around 1818. [MCA]

GORDON, JOHN, a white ironsmith, was admitted as a burgess of Arbroath in 1797. [AA.18.941]

GORDON, JOHN, from Arbroath, a theological student in 1808, emigrated to Canada, later an agriculturalist. [UPC]

GORDON, JOHN, from Angus, graduated MA from King's College, Aberdeen, on 31 March 1809S. [KCA]

GORDON, PETER, from Brechin, a theological student in 1800, later a minister in St John's, New Brunswick. [UPC]

GORDON, PETER, of Dickmontlaw, St Vigeans, was accused of assaulting a Revenue officer in 1812. [NRS.JC26.1812.11]

GORDON, THOMAS, a merchant in Madeira, a sasine 1782. [NRS.Forfar.127]

GORDON, WILLIAM, son of William Gordon of Blelack, Dundee, a student in Marischal College, Aberdeen, in 1790s. [MCA]

GORDON, WILLIAM, born 1810, third son of William Gordon a vintner in Montrose, a joiner who died in New Orleans, Louisiana, on 27 September 1835. [AJ.4587]

GOURLAY, DAVID, born 1752, a shipmaster in Arbroath, died in 1840, husband of Jean Clark. [Arbroath Abbey gravestone]

GOURLAY, GERSHOM, of Baikie, born 1752, died in Dundee on 9 December 1825. [SM.97.128]

GOURLAY, JAMES, a merchant in Dundee, son of John Gourlay a glover there, 1798. [DCA.B19.3.27/15]

GOURLAY, JANET, born 1749, died in 1804. [Arbroath Abbey gravestone]

GOW, GEORGE, a merchant, was admitted as a burgess of Arbroath in 1790. [AA.18.941]

GOW, JAMES, a merchant, was admitted as a burgess of Arbroath in 1797. [AA.18.941]

GOW, JOHN, a merchant, was admitted as a burgess of Arbroath in 1797. [AA.18.941]

GOW, WILLIAM, a merchant, was admitted as a burgess of Arbroath in 1794. [AA.18.941]

GOW, HARRIS, and Company, tanners in Arbroath, 1797. [NRS.CS230.Seqn.G1.9]

GOWANS, ALEXANDER, a millwright, was admitted as a burgess of Arbroath in 1797. [AA.18.941]

GOWANS, Reverend JOHN, in Lunan, was admitted as a burgess of Arbroath in 1791. [AA.18.941]

GOWANS, JOHN, a skipper in Horse Wynd, Dundee, in 1818, master of the Expedition, [DD]; master of the Fishers of Dundee in 1824, and of the Augusta of Dundee in 1825. [DSR]

GOWANS, THOMAS, a baker, was admitted as a burgess of Arbroath in 1795. [AA.18.941]

GOWANS, WILLIAM, born 1725, died 1797, husband of Elizabeth Mustard, born 1729, died 1767. [Howff gravestone, Dundee]

GOWRIE, DAVID, a shoemaker, was admitted as a burgess of Arbroath in 1797. [AA.18.941]

GRAHAM, GEORGE, son of Peter Graham a shoemaker in Kirriemuir, a student at Marischal College, Aberdeen, in 1851, a United Presbyterian minister in Stornaway, later in Queensland, Australia. [MCA]

GRAHAM, JAMES, of Meathie, testament, 9 November 1792, Comm. Brechin. [NRS]

GRAHAM, JAMES, a weaver in Seafield Lane, Dundee, was accused of mobbing and rioting in the New Hall, Bell Street, Dundee, in 1842. [NRS.AD14.42.354; JC26.1843.443]

GRAHAM, ROBERT STIRLING, of Kincaldrum, versus Graham Bower in 1818. [NRS.CS271.57863]

GRAHAM, ROBERT WILLIAM, of Morphie, testaments, 1793/1794, Comm. Brechin. [NRS]

GRANDISON, ROBERT, born 1788, a wright at the West Port, Dundee, was accused of theft in 1830. [NRS.AD14.30.90; JC26.1830.17]

GRANT, DAVID, a merchant, was admitted as a burgess of Arbroath in 1794. [AA.18.941]

GRANT, FERGUS, a weaver, was admitted as a burgess of Arbroath in 1791. [AA.18.941]

GRANT, FREDERICK, born 1779, from Quebec, died at Mount Cyrus, Montrose, on 1 November 1842. [GM.NS19.109]

GRANT, GEORGE, a barber, was admitted as a burgess of Arbroath in 1796. [AA.18.941]

GRANT, GEORGE COLE, a surgeon, seventh son of Reverend Dr Alexander Grant in Dundee, died in Jamaica in June 1801, testament, 1802, Comm. Edinburgh. [NRS] [GM.71.960] [GC.1577]

GRANT, HARRY, a merchant in Charleston, South Carolina, appointed James Carnegie Lindsay of Kinblethmont, Angus, as his attorney in 1792. [NRS.RD4.252.1272]

GRANT, Reverend PETER, and his wife Helen Guillan in Dundee, parents of Peter Guillan Grant, born 21 January 1862, died in Victoria, British Columbia, on 16 May 1897. [F.3.329]

GRANT, WILLIAM, a merchant, was admitted as a burgess of Arbroath in 1796. [AA.18.941]

GRAY, JAMES, born 1762, a merchant in Dundee, died 1826. [DCA.B19.3.27/210] [Howff gravestone, Dundee]

GRAY, JAMES, master aboard the Friendship of Dundee at the Davis Straits in 1824. [NRS.E508.130.8]

GRAY, JAMES, a confectioner in Dundee, a tack, 1840. [NRS.GD45.16]

GRAY, JOHN, at Witch's know, Dundee, was accused of theft in the parish of Mains and Strathmartine in 1822. [NRS.AD14.22.67]

GRAY, PATRICK, probably from Glamis, settled at Montego Bay and at Hanover, Jamaica, administration, 1807, London. [TNA.Prob.11.1459]

GRAY, ROBERT, keeper of the Tolbooth of Dundee in 1798. [DCA.B19.2.27/5]

GRAY, ROBERT, born 1782, a surgeon, died in Jamaica on 25 June 1812. [Constitution Road gravestone, Dundee]

GRAY, ROBERT A., son of Robert Gray a carpenter in Airlie, graduated MA, at Marischal College, Aberdeen, in 1834. [MCA]

GRAY, SAMUEL, born 23 December 1794 in Dundee, died in Serampore, Bengal, India, on 14 December 1820. [Danish Cemetery, gravestone, Serampore]

GRAY, THOMAS, a skipper in the Seagait of Dundee and master of the Lord Kinnaird in 1818, [DD], and of the Perth of Dundee in 1824. [DSR]

GRAY, WILLIAM, of Balgarno, testament, 1794, Comm. Brechin. [NRS]

GRAY, WILLIAM, was admitted as a burgess of Arbroath in 1798. [AA.18.941]

GRAY, WILLIAM, born 1801, a railway engineman of the Dundee and Newtyle Railway Company, Hatton Hill, Newtyle, was accused of culpable homicide in 1836. [NRS.AD14.36.89]

GREENHILL, ALEXANDER, in Fearn, papers, 1828-1829. [NRS.GD16.27.327]

GREENHILL, MARY, born 1772, died 1794. [Howff gravestone, Dundee]

GREENHILL, PATRICK, born 1723, died 1792, and daughter Margaret Greenhill, born 1772, died 1794. [Howff gravestone, Dundee]

GREIG, ALEXANDER, born 1727, a wine merchant in Montrose, died in 1805. [Maryton gravestone]

GREIG, DAVID, a landowner in 1770, Provost of Arbroath, a merchant there by 1797, husband of Magdalene Black, born 1739, died 1782. [NRS.RS35.24.122; GD45.16.278][DLS.26]

GREIG, JAMES, from Forfar, graduated MA from King's College, Aberdeen, in March 1832. [KCA]

GREIG, JANE, born 1797, died 1838, wife of Alexander Gouk a blacksmith in Montrose. [Montrose, Episcopal gravestone]

GREIG, ROBERT, a weaver, was admitted as a burgess of Arbroath in 1797. [AA.18.941]

GREIG, ROBERT, from Inverkeillor, a student in Marischal College in 1790s. [MCA]

GRIEVE, PHILIP, sailor aboard the Princess Charlotte of Dundee bound for the Davis Strait in 1824. [NRS.E508.129.8]

GRIGORY, JAMES, master of the Bruce of Dundee trading between Riga, Latvia, and Dundee in 1818. [NRS.E504.11.21]

GROAT, JOHN, apprentice aboard the Estridge of Dundee bound for the Davis Straits in 1824. [NRS.E508.129.8]

GROOL, ALEXANDER, a shipmaster, was admitted as a burgess of Arbroath in 1798. [AA.18.941]

GUILD, ALEXANDER, born 1795 in Arbroath, a clerk in Skinner's Close, Edinburgh, accused of theft and reset in 1830. [NRS.AD14.30.343]

GUILD, ALEXANDER, born 28 April 1826 in Dundee, son of John Guild, a linen merchant in New York who died in the Hotel Vendome on 5 November 1893. [ANY.2.237]

GUILD, DAVID, born 1795, a merchant who died in Philadelphia, Pennsylvania, on 5 March 1830. [Howff gravestone, Dundee]

GUILD, GEORGE, a shoemaker, was admitted as a burgess of Arbroath in 1798. [AA.18.941]

GUILD, JAMES, in Muirdrum, was accused of forgery, but failed to appear in court so was outlawed in 1832. [NRS.JC26.1832.313]

GUILD, JAMES F., born 1825, died in Melbourne, Australia, on 8 January 1866. [Howff gravestone, Dundee]

GUILD, WILLIAM, in Jamaica, son of Provost John Guild, was admitted as a burgess of Dundee on 18 September 1817. [DBR]

GUILLAN, ALEXANDER, born 1813, son of David Guillan and his wife Ann Gardner, died in the Bass Strait, Tasmania, Australia, on 5 September 1848. [Howff gravestone, Dundee]

GUILLAN, DAVID, a brewer in Dundee, 1798. [DCA.B19.3.27/1]

GUILLAN, JOHN, born 1806, died in Launceston, Van Diemen's Land, [Tasmania], Australia, on 20 April 1851. [Howff gravestone, Dundee]

GUNN, JAMES, born 1842, son of James Gunn and his wife Isabel Smith, died in Australia on 10 January 1863. [St Vigeans gravestone]

GUTHRIE, ANN, in Canada, joint-heir of Charles Winter in Craigend of Auldbar in 1824. [NRS.S/H]

GUTHRIE, JAMES, a distiller at Easterton of Dunlappy, sederunt book, 1833-1838. [NRS.CS96.4667-4670]

GUTHRIE, JOHN, born 1739, a merchant in Dundee, died 1786, testament, 1786, Comm. Brechin. [NRS]; husband of Helen Yeaman, born 1755, died 1818. [Howff gravestone, Dundee]

GUTHRIE, JOHN, in Hilltown, Dundee, son of John Guthrie, 1798. [DCA.B19.3.27/181]

GUTHRIE, PATRICK, born 8 October 1776 in Dundee, son of John Guthrie and his wife Helen Yeaman, a merchant in Jamaica, a deed, 1818. [NRS.RD5.144.504]; died at Montego Bay on 21 December 1821. [Montego Bay gravestone, Jamaica]

GUTHRIE, THOMAS, a merchant in Dundee, testament, 1795, Comm. Brechin. [NRS]

GUTHRIE, THOMAS, born 1736, a merchant in Dundee, died 1813, husband of Jean Pyot, born 1738, died 1806. [Howff gravestone, Dundee]

GUTHRIE, WILLIAM, in Canada, joint-heir of Charles Winter in Craigend of Auldbar in 1824. [NRS.S/H]

GUTHRIE and BAXTER, merchants in Dundee trading with Baltic ports in 1836-1837. [NRS.CS96.4738]

HACKNEY, JOHN, a merchant in Westhaven of Panbride, testament, 1800, Comm. Brechin. [NRS]

HADDEN, JAMES, in Aberdeen, was admitted as a burgess of Arbroath in 1791. [AA.18.941]

HADDEN, JAMES, was admitted as a burgess of Arbroath in 1794. [AA.18.941]

HAIG, WILLIAM, a merchant, was admitted as a burgess of Arbroath in 1796. [AA.18.941]

HAIR, GEORGE, a merchant in Dundee, testament, 1800, Comm. Brechin. [NRS]

HALKETT, PETER, tenant in Pitcur, sederunt book, 1842. [NRS.CS96.4395]

HALLEY, WILLIAM, jr., born 1824, died in Dunedin, New Zealand, on 21 July 1890. [Western gravestone, Dundee]

HALIBURTON, JAMES, born 1730, a magistrate of Dundee, died 1802. [Howff gravestone, Dundee]

HALLIBURTON, JOHN, a sailor of the Friendship of Dundee at the Davis Straits in 1824. [NRS.E508.130.8]

HALIBURTON, THOMAS, on the Prince of Wales Island, later in Dundee, testament, 9 August 1823. [NRS.CC3.3.16.40]

HALLIBURTON, WILLIAM, son of John Halliburton of Muirton the Customs Controller of Dundee, a disposition, 1800. [NRS.GD1.197.15]

HALLIDAY, JOHN, a salmon fisher at West Ferry, a Precept of Removal, 1815. [NRS.GD45.18.2358]

HAMILTON, ROBERT, born 1714, a mason in Dundee, died 1802, husband of Jean Strang, born 1716, died 1773. [Howff gravestone, Dundee]

HANLEY, FRANCIS, master of the George of Dundee from Dundee via Cromarty etc with passengers bound for Pictou, Quebec and Montreal in 1843, similarly in 1850. [LCL.29.3174] [DPCA.2128][BPP]

HARBEN, EMILY, born 1815, died in Westport, New Zealand, on 13 May 1888. [Western gravestone, Dundee]

HARDIE, JAMES, in Blackhill, Bridestone, Kirriemuir, was the victim of assault and murder in 1831. [NRS.AD14.31.18]

HARDIE, JOHN, a labourer in West Muir, Kirriemuir, was accused of assault and murder in 1831. [NRS.AD14.31.1]

HARRIS, GEORGE, sailor aboard the Princess Charlotte of Dundee bound for the Davis Strait in 1824. [NRS.E508.129.8]

HARVEY, ARTHUR, son of John Harvey of Kinnettles, a student at Marischal College, Aberdeen, in 1820s, later settled in Natal, South Africa. [MCA]

HARVEY, JOHN, son of John Harvey of Kinnettles, a student at Marischal College, Aberdeen, in 1820, later in the service of the East India Company. [MCA]

HARVEY, ROBERT, son of John Harvey of Kinnettles, a student at Marischal College, Aberdeen, in 1830s. [MCA]

HARVEY, THOMAS, son of John Harvey of Kinnettles, a student at Marischal College, Aberdeen, in 1820s. [MCA]

HASTINGS, ALEXANDER, a weaver, was admitted as a burgess of Arbroath in 1797. [AA.18.941]

HAY, CATHERINE, daughter of William Hay a merchant in Montrose, testament 21 December 1797, Comm. Brechin. [NRS]

HAY, DANIEL, son of James Hay a merchant in Dundee, died in Philadelphia, Pennsylvania, on 4 July 1797.

HAY, DAVID, the younger, a weaver, was admitted as a burgess of Arbroath in 1797. [AA.10.101]

HAY, JAMES, a merchant, was admitted as a burgess of Arbroath in 1798. [AA.18.941]

HAY, JAMES, a writer in Dundee, testament, 1798, Comm. Brechin. [NRS]

HAY, JAMES, born 1800, a farmer who emigrated from Dundee on the brig Traveller of Aberdeen bound for South Carolina in 1822. [NARA]

HAY, JAMES, son of James Hay a schoolmaster in Montrose, graduated MA from Marischal College, Aberdeen, in 1839, later a minister. [MCA]

HAY, Dr JOHN, in Grenada, was admitted as a burgess of Arbroath in 1790. [AA.18.941]

HAY, JOHN, a tailor, was admitted as a burgess of Arbroath in 1798. [AA.18.941]

HAY, MARY, in Lochside, Montrose, was accused of mobbing and rioting there in 1813. [NRS.AD14.13.84]

HAYDEN, JAMES, born 1773, a farmer, with his wife Elizabeth born 1775, and eight children, who emigrated from Dundee on the brig Trafalgar bound for Charleston, South Carolina, in 1823. [NARA]

HAZEEL, DAVID, a manufacturer in Dundee, 1799. [DCA.B19.3.27/233]

HEADRICK, Dr WILLIAM, fourth son of Reverend James Headrick in Dunnichen, died on Blue Hole Estate, Hanover, Jamaica, on 17 December 1848. [EEC.21784] [AJ.5280]

HENDERSON, ALEXANDER, from Angus, graduated MA from King's College, Aberdeen, on 31 March 1827, later an Episcopal minister in Hamilton, Lanarkshire. [KCA]

HENDERSON, JAMES O., and his sons James Henderson and Charles in Rochilhill farm, Glamis, a deed, 1803. [NRS.CS237.H2.28.1]

HENDERSON, JAMES, a baker and confectioner in Brechin, 1845. [NRS.CS280.7.24]

HENDERSON, JOHN, a skipper in Fish Street, Dundee, master of the Cygnet of Dundee from 1815 to 1820, [DPCA.685/770] [NRS.E504.11.20-21], trading between Memel, Lithuania, and Dundee in 1819, also between Dundee and Quebec and Montreal in 1820. [NRS.E504.11.21]; and of the Williams of Dundee in 1825, [DSR], master of the Ossian of Dundee trading between Memel, Lithuania, and Dundee in 1831. [MD.116]; testament, 1834. [NRS.SC45.31.2.218

HENDERSON, JOHN, MD, a surgeon of the Bengal Establishment, died at Lodiana on the banks of the Satlaj, India, on 12 March 1836. [St Vigeans gravestone]

HENDERSON, Dr ROBERT, born 1750, a physician in Dundee, died 1824, husband of Ann ..., born 1759, died 1808. [Howff gravestone, Dundee]

HENDERSON, THOMAS, a weaver in Dundee, testament, 1796, Comm. Brechin. [NRS]

HENDERSON, WILLIAM, son of Dr Henderson in Dundee, died in Quito, Ecuador, in November 1822. [BM.14.624]

HENDERSON, WILLIAM, graduated MA from King's College, Aberdeen, on 27 November 1826, later an Episcopal minister in Arbroath. [KCA]

HENDRY, MATHEW, acting mate of the Friendship of Dundee at the Davis Straits in 1824. [NRS.E508.130.8]

HENRY, Dr JOHN, in St Croix, Danish West Indies, was admitted as a burgess of Arbroath in 1791. [ArBR]

HENRY, THOMAS, in Lochee, parish of Liff, testament, 1796, Comm. St Andrews. [NRS]

HEPBURN, ROBERT, a shipmaster in Errol, later a mariner in Dundee, testament, 1804. [NRS.CC3.13.137]

HERALD, ANDREW, born 1832, son of George Herald and his wife Catherine Kydd, died in South Trees Port, Queensland, Australia, on 10 November 1876. [Arbroath Abbey gravestone]

HERALD, DAVID, in Lidnathy, Kirriemuir, testament, 1791, Comm. St Andrews. [NRS]

HERALD, JAMES, son of John Herald a weaver in Kirriemuir, a student at Marischal College, Aberdeen, in 1845, a Presbyterian minister in Canada. [MCA]

HERD, JOHN, master of the Favourite of Dundee in 1809. [DD]

HEWAN, THOMAS, formerly of the 4$^{th}$ Dragoons, later Captain of the Angus Fencibles, and his wife Elisabeth Leslie, parents of John Hewan in Orangehill, Jamaica, in 1815. [NRS.RD5.98.389]

HILL, ABRAM, born 1732, died 1816, husband of Effie Mitchell, born 1728, died 1811. [Howff gravestone, Dundee]

HILL, ALEXANDER, a gardener in Dundee, testament, 1791, Comm. Brechin. [NRS]

HILL, JAMES, born 1778, a weaver in Dundee who was murdered in Chapelshade, Dundee, in 1799. [Howff gravestone, Dundee]

HILL, JAMES, an apprentice aboard the Dorothy of Dundee bound for the Davis Straits in 1825. [NRS.E508.130.8]

HILL, JAMES, son of David Hill a merchant in Dundee, a student at Marischal College, Aberdeen, in 1840, emigrated to New Zealand. [MCA]

HILL, JOHN, from Arbroath, graduated MA from King's College, Aberdeen, on 26 April 1813. [KCA]

HOBART, THOMAS, son of James Hobart an architect in Kirriemuir, graduated MA at Marischal College in 1848, later a minister of the Original Secession Curch in Carluke, Lanarkshire. [MCA]

HODGETON, WILLIAM, son of John Hodgeton a wright in Arbroath, a student at Marischal College, Aberdeen, in 1820s. [MCA]

HOGG, ALEXANDER, a slater in Panbride, a tack, 1840. [NRS.GD45.16]

HOGG, ALEXANDER, a child of John Hogg a skipper in Montrose, in 1848. [NRS.CS313.733]

HOME, DAVID JAMES, and his wife Augusta, of Dundee, parents of Frederick James Home, born 1852, died in New Orleans, Louisiana, on 19 September 1878. [S.10998]

HOOD, FREDERICK, at the West Port of Dundee, testament, 1796. Comm. Brechin. [NRS]

HOOD, JOHN, a sailor aboard the Friendship of Dundee at the Davis Straits in 1824. [NRS.E508.130.8]

HOOD, MARGARET, died in Quebec on 3 November 1861. [Howff gravestone, Dundee]

HOW, ANDREW, born 1781, a skipper in the Overgait, Dundee, 1818, [DD], master of the Alert of Dundee in 1795, of the Margaret of Dundee in 1797, [NRS.CE70.1.8/58, 77], of the Hector of Dundee in 1808, [DPCA.710][DD], died in 1841, testament, [NRS.SC46.31.6.1]

HOWE, DAVID, from Angus, graduated MA from King's College, Aberdeen, on 30 March 1790. [KCA]

HOW, DAVID, born 1754, a merchant in Dundee, died 1794, husband of Eliza Doig. [Howff gravestone, Dundee]

HOW, WILLIAM, in Milltown of Cortachy, a tack, 1800. [NRS.GD16.28.471]

HOWDEN, ARTHUR, in Elsinore, Denmark, was admitted as a burgess of Arbroath in 1791. [ArBR]

HOWIE, CHARLES, from Kirriemuir, graduated MA from King's College, Aberdeen, in March 1854, later a schoolmaster in Kirriemuir. [KCA]

HOWIE, DAVID, born 1758, a shipmaster in Peter Street, Dundee, 1809, 1818, [DD]; master of the Lively of Dundee in 1797, of the London Packet of Dundee in1799, [NRS.CE70.1.8/52]; of the Osnaburg of Dundee in 1818. [DD], died in 1832. [Howff gravestone]

HUDSON, Captain, master of the Emma of Dundee from the River Clyde to Quebec in 1836. [GA.5182]

HUME, JAMES HILL, born 1830, a baker, died in South Yarra, Melbourne, Australia, on 12 October 1887. [St Aidan's gravestone, Broughty Ferry]

HUNTER, ALEXANDER GIBSON, of the Links of Barry, 1810. [NRS.RHP.1142]

HUNTER, DAVID, a merchant in Dundee, 1798. [DCA.B19.3.27/4]

HUNTER, JAMES, born 1782 in Montrose, a merchant in Charleston, South Carolina, was naturalised there on 22 August 1810. [NARA.M1183.1]

HUNTER, JOHN, third son of Charles Hunter of Burnside in Angus, died on Horseshoe Plantation, South Carolina, in 1824. [EA]

HUNTER, MCNAUGHTON, MD, born 1733, a physician in Montrose, died 14 March 1830. [Montrose gravestone]

HUNTER, ROBERT, Acting Customs Controller of Dundee in 1820. [NRS.E504.11.21]

HUNTER, SUSAN, wife of William Brown a mariner in Stobswell, Arbroath, was found guilty of malicious mischief and sentenced to four months imprisonment in Arbroath in 1843. [NRS.JC26.1843.156]

HUNTER, WILLIAM, a carrier, was admitted as a burgess of Arbroath in 1794. [AA.18.941]

HUNTER, WILLIAM, a merchant in Forfar, testament, 1794, Comm. St Andrews. [NRS]

HUSBAND, JAMES, a merchant, was admitted as a burgess of Arbroath in 1794. [AA.18.941]

HUSSEY, JAMES, a wright in Bonnyton, Arbirlot, died aged 70, he was married in 1776 to Elizabeth Ferrier, born 1745, died 1815, parents of Elizabeth Hussey born 1778, died 1816. [Arbirlot gravestone]

HUTCHEON, ALEXANDER, a butcher, was admitted as a burgess of Arbroath in 1794. [AA.18.941]

HUTCHEN, JAMES, born 1811, died in Talbot, Australia, on 20 December 1877. [Rosehill gravestone, Montrose]

HUTCHEON, GEORGE, born 1822, son of William Hutcheon and his wife Catherine Hickton, died in Port Adelaide, South Australia, on 18 April 1858. [Montrose gravestone]

HUTCHISON, JAMES, a fresh or green man aboard the Friendship of Dundee at the Davis Straits in 1824. [NRS.E508.130.8]

HUTT, THOMAS, harpooner aboard the Princess Charlotte of Dundee, bound for the Davis Strait in 1824. [NRS.E508.129.8]

HUTTON, AGNES, born 1813, wife of John Cromarty a sailor in Marketgait, Arbroath, was accused of the murder of her husband in 1843. [NRS.AD14.43.373]

HUTTON, ALEXANDER, a journeyman shoemaker in Overgait, Dundee, was accused of membership of an unlawful combination, in 1820. [NRS.AD14.20.215]

HUTTON, ANDREW, a skipper on the Shore, Dundee in 1782, [DD], master of the Isabella of Dundee in 1809. [DD]

HUTTON, DAVID, a shipmaster in Dundee, died 1793, husband of Isobel Henderson, born 1746, died 1809. [Howff gravestone, Dundee]

HUTTON, GEORGE, sailor aboard the Estridge of Dundee, bound for the Davis Straits in 1824. [NRS.E508.129.8]

HUTTON, ROBERT, a shipmaster in Dundee, testament, 1799, Comm. Brechin. [NRS]

IDLE, Mrs BIDAH, a tenant in Careston, in 1834. [NRS.CS.46.1833.174]

INGLIS, DAVID, from Angus, graduated MA from King's College, Aberdeen, on 30 March 1797, later minister at Leochel. [KCA]

INGLIS, ROBERT, from Angus, graduated MA from King's College, Aberdeen, on 30 March 1821, later was the minister of St Luke's in British Guiana. [KCA]

INNES, ALEXANDER, master of the Emma of Dundee, from Dundee with passengers bound for Quebec in 1842. [BPP]; from Dundee to Montreal in 1843. [DW]

INNES, DAVID, born 1796, farmer at Arsallary, died 2 September 1865, husband of Martha Christieson, born 1806, died 7 February 1894. [Lochlee gravestone]

INNES, Mrs, wife of Captain Innes of the Forfar Militia, died in Montrose on 25 November 1825. [SM.97.127]

INVERARITY, JAMES, a merchant and tanner in Brechin, testament, 1795, Comm. Brechin. [NRS]

INVERARITY, JAMES, son of David Inverarity a merchant in Arbroath, a student in Marischal College, Aberdeen, in 1790s, later a surgeon in the service of the East India Company. [MCA]

INVERARITY, JOHN, born 1749 in Brechin, a tanner, emigrated by 1792, a partner in Panton, Leslie and Company in Pensacola, Florida, and in Savannah, Georgia, died in London in 1805, admin.1805, PCC. [TNA] [Indian Traders of the south-east Spanish Borderlands, 1986]

IRELAND, GEORGE, born 1839, died in San Francisco, California, on 3 February 1864. [Western gravestone, Dundee]

IRELAND, JAMES, a mason in Keillor, Newtyle, testament, 1800, Comm. St Andrews. [NRS]

IRELAND, JAMES, born 1773, a skipper on Yeaman Shore, Dundee, master of the Rodney of Dundee in 1809, and of the Friendship of Dundee in 1818, at the Davis Straits in 1824, [NRS.E508.130.8]; died at sea in 1824. [Howff gravestone, Dundee]

IRELAND, JAMES, fresh or green man aboard the Princess Charlotte of Dundee bound for the Davis Strait in 1824. [NRS.E508.129.8]

IRELAND, JOHN, a bookseller, was admitted as a burgess of Arbroath in 1797. [AA.18.941]

IRELAND, WILLIAM, fresh or green man aboard the Princess Charlotte of Dundee bound for the Davis Strait in 1824. [NRS.E508.129.8]

IRELAND, WILLIAM, born 1825, son of John Ireland, died in Hobartown, Tasmania, Australia, on 19 September 1862. [Western gravestone, Dundee]

IRINSIE, Major NINIAN, was admitted as a burgess of Arbroath in 1795. [AA.18.941]

IRONS, EUPHAN, daughter of Robert Irons a weaver in Dundee, versus James White a druggist in Arbroath, a Process of Divorce in 1816. [NRS.CC8.6.1620]

IRONS, MARTIN, sailor aboard the Estridge of Dundee bound for the Davis Straits in 1824. [NRS.E508.129.8]

IRONS, ROBERT, line manager aboard the Princess Charlotte of Dundee bound for the Davis Strait in 1824. [NRS.E508.129.8]

IVORY, JAMES, a flax spinner in Douglastown, trading with Baltic ports from 1799 to 1803. [NRS.CS96.3843]

IRVINE, ROBERT, a shoemaker, was admitted as a burgess of Arbroath in 1798. [AA.18.941]

JACK, DAVID, a skipper in the Vault, Dundee, in 1818, master of the John in 1818, [DD]; and of the Choice of Dundee in 1824. DSR], [DD]

JACK, HENRY, born 1737, died 1806, husband of Jean Hunter, born 1741, died 1830. [Howff gravestone, Dundee]

JACK, JOHN, born 1757, a shipmaster in Arbroath, died 1801, husband of Jean Brown. [Arbroath Abbey gravestone]

JACK, JOHN, a weaver, was admitted as a burgess of Arbroath in 1797. [AA.18.941]

JACK, JOHN, master of the John of Dundee trading between Riga, Latvia, and Dundee in 1819. [NRS.E504.11.21]

JAMIE, DAVID, at Law of Craigie, Logie Pert, testament, 1800, Comm. St Andrews. [NRS]

JAMIESON, AGNES, a widow in Fotheringham, Inverarity, a victim of a mob and rioters in the New Hall, Bell Street, Dundee, in 1842. [NRS.AD14.42.354; JC26.1843.443]

JAMIESON, DAVID, a wright in Dundee, testament, 1798, Comm. Brechin. [NRS]

JAMIESON, JOHN, steersman aboard the Princess Charlotte of Dundee bound for the Davis Strait in 1824. [NRS.E508.129.8]

JAMIESON, JOSEPH, harpooner aboard the Estridge of Dundee, bound for the Davis Straits in 1824. [NRS.E508.129.8]

JAPP, ALEXANDER, master of the Dame of Dundee trading between Leith and Dundee in 1819. [NRS.E504.11.21]

JAPP, MARGARET, widow of Alexander Law a shipmaster in Montrose, testament, 1795, Comm. Brechin. [NRS]

JAPP, ROBERT, born 1724, son of John Japp, died in 1807. [Montrose gravestone]

JARRON, DAVID, a hay-dresser, was admitted as a burgess of Arbroath in 1797. [AA.18.941]

JARRON, GEORGE, son of George Jarron in Balviny, Aberlemno, a student at Marischal College, Aberdeen, around 1817. [MCA]

JARRON, MARGARET, born 1732, died 1799, wife of Henry Petrie a burgess of Arbroath. [Arbroath Abbey gravestone]

JARVIS, ROBERT, a merchant, was admitted as a burgess of Arbroath in 1792. [AA.18.941]

JAY, JOHN, a merchant in Rotterdam, Zealand, was admitted as a burgess of Arbroath in 1791. [AA.18.941]

JEFFERSON, JOHN, [1806-1847], and his wife Eliza Ogilvy, [1813-1863], parents of David Jefferson, a shipmaster who was drowned at San Francisco, California, on 16 September 1893, and was buried at Laurel Hill cemetery there. [Arbroath Abbey gravestone]

JENKINS, JAMES, in Millhead, Arbroath, a victim of theft in 1832. [NRS.AD14.32.130]

JIFFERS, WILLIAM, master of the Horn of Dundee in 1824. [DD]

JOBSON, ANDREW, a merchant tailor in Dundee, 1799. [DCA.B19.3.27/266]

JOBSON, DAVID, a writer in Dundee, testament, 1791, Comm. Brechin. [NRS][NRS.CS16.1.125/250][DCA.B19.3.27/11]

JOHNSTON, ALEXANDER, born 1776, Sergeant Major of the Forfar and Kincardine Militia, died on 28 May 1836. [Montrose gravestone]

JOHNSTON, ANN, born 1798, wife of William Stewart, died in Andover, Massachusetts, on 1 September 1855. [Farnell gravestone]

JOHNSTON, CHARLES, a wright, was admitted as a burgess of Arbroath in 1791. [AA.18.941]

JOHNSTON, GEORGE, a wright, was admitted as a burgess of Arbroath in 1797. [AA.18.941]

JOHNSTONE, HENRY, born 1771, a merchant in Bain's Square, Dundee, died 25 February 1809. [DE.41]

JOHNSTONE, JAMES, a surgeon and former Provost of Dundee, testament, 1799, Comm. Brechin. [NRS]

JOHNSTONE, JAMES, a surgeon in the Service of the Honourable East India Company, son of Provost James Johnstone of Dundee, was admitted as a burgess of Dundee in 1799. [DBR]

JOHNSTON, JAMES, born 1731, a linen manufacturer and Provost of Arbroath, died 29 October 1806, husband of Ann Anderson, born 1738, died 1786. [Arbroath Abbey gravestone] [NRS.E326.1.133]

JOHNSTON, JOHN, in Crudie, a burgess of Arbroath in 1790. [AA.18.941]

JOHNSTON, ROBERT, born 1755, died 1806, husband of Agnes Ross. [Howff gravestone, Dundee]

JOHNSTON, THOMAS, master of the Helen of Montrose from Montrose with passengers to Quebec in 1849, 1850, 1852, 1853, and 1854. [EEC][LCL]

JOLLY, ALEXANDER, applied for a tack of the sheep farm of Waterhead in the parish of Lethnott and Navar in 1816. [NRS.GD45.18.2021]

JOLLY, ALEXANDER, born 1818, son of James Jolly and his wife Jean Robie, died in Geelong, Australia, on 29 March 1840. [Brechin gravestone]

JOLLY, JOHN, a sailor aboard the Friendship of Dundee at the Davis Straits in 1824. [NRS.E508.130.8]

JOLLY, JOHN, father of William Jolly, born 1853, a carpenter who died in Melbourne, Australia, on 6 July 1878. [Rosehill gravestone, Montrose]

JOLLY, Reverend PETER, '57 years Episcopal clergyman at Lochlee', husband of Jean Diack, born 1753, died 12 May 1809, parents of James Jolly, born 1788, died 14 March 1798. [Lochlee gravestone]

JOLLY, WILLIAM, son of Alexander Jolly in Glenesk, a student at Marischal College, Aberdeen in 1809. [MCA]

JUST, JAMES, master of the Isabella of Dundee from Dundee to Quebec in 1841, 1842. [QM][DPCA]

JUST, THOMAS, from Dundee, graduated MA from King's College, Aberdeen, in March 1846. [KCA]

KANDOW, JAMES, in Roughhaugh, Lintrathen, testament, 1793, Comm. St Andrews. [NRS]

KEAY, DAVID, born 1725, a shipmaster in Dundee, died 1807, husband of Susanna Bower, born 1744, died 1805. [Howff gravestone, Dundee]; master of the Hope of Dundee trading between St Petersburg, Russia, and Dundee in 1818. [NRS.E504.11.21]

KEAY, DAVID, jr., born 1761, a shipmaster in the Nethergait, Dundee, in 1809, master of the Swift of Dundee in 1809, and of the Hope of Dundee in 1824, [DSR], died in 1843. [Howff gravestone, Dundee]

KEILL, JAMES, born 1733, a gunner in the Royal Navy, died 1816, husband of Elizabeth Cargill. [Arbroath Abbey gravestone]

KEILLER, ALEXANDER BENNET, born in 1824, son of John Keiller and his wife Ann Bennet, died in Tobago on 27 April 1848. [Howff gravestone, Dundee]

KEILLER, GEORGE, a skipper burgess of Dundee in 1797, [DBR], master of the Diamond of Dundee in 1797, [NRS.CE70.1.8.61]; testament, 1803, [NRS.CC3.13.66]

KEILLER, JEAN, in Marywell, St Vigeans, was accused of child murder but found not guilty in 1850. [NRS.JC26.1850.739]

KEILLER, JESSIE BENNET, born 1802, wife of Robert Hood a merchant in Missouri, died in Dundee on 24 May 1843, [Howff gravestone, Dundee]

KEILLER, MARGARET, born 1800, daughter of James Keiller, [1759-1846], a merchant in Dundee, wife of Archibald McGowan MD, died in Portland, Jamaica, on 29 November 1822. [Howff gravestone, Dundee] [Machineal gravestone, Jamaica]

KEILLER, MUNGO, a porter in Dundee in 1796. [DCA.B19.3.26/1]

KEILLER, PETER, a sailor aboard the Friendship of Dundee at the Davis Straits in 1824. [NRS.E508.130.8]

KEIR, ANDREW, born 1832, son of William Keir and his wife Catherine Smith, died in Ballarat, Australia, on 7 August 1859. [Western gravestone, Dundee]

KEIR, ELSPETH, born 1715, died 1792. [Howff gravestone, Dundee]

KEIR, GEORGE, a burgess of Arbroath in 1791. [AA.18.941]

KEITH, ALEXANDER, a tailor, who was admitted as a burgess of Arbroath in 1791. [AA.18.941]

KEITH, DAVID, born 1758, a shipmaster in Arbroath in 1778, died in 1821. [NRS.S/H][Arbroath Abbey gravestone]

KEITH, GEORGE, a merchant from Charleston, South Carolina, was granted the lands of Ulysseshaven and those of Scotstoun in 1817. [NRS.RGS.155/66; RS.Forfar.282]

KEITH, GEORGE, a fresh or green man aboard the <u>Estridge of Dundee,</u> bound for the Davis Straits in 1824. [NRS.E508.129.8]

KEITH, JAMES, born 1756, an accountant, died in Dundee on 2 December 1825. [SM.97.127]

KEITH, JOHN, born 1769, a shipmaster in Montrose, died in Riga, Latvia, in 1822. [Inchbrioch gravestone]

KEITH, SUSANNA, daughter of James Keith the Excise collector in Dundee, married James Allardyce of St Vincent, British West Indies, in Dundee on 1 November 1796. [SM.58.791]

KEITH, WILLIAM, from Arbroath, graduated MA from King's College, Aberdeen, in March 1858, later a Free Church minister in Arbroath. [KCA]

KENNEDY, ALEXANDER, from Dundee, graduated MA from King's College, Aberdeen, in April 1859, later a minister in Stewarton and in Edinburgh. [KCA]

KENNEDY, JOHN, a skipper on the West Shore in 1782, and in Fish Street, Dundee, in 1809, [DD]; was admitted as a burgess of Dundee in 1796. [DBR]

KENNEDY, JOHN, born 1848, son of James Kennedy and his wife Margaret Spalding, died in Redwood City, California, on 20 April 1890. [Kirriemuir gravestone]

KENNY, CHARLES, a mariner in Arbroath, testament, 1803, Comm. St Andrews. [NRS]

KERR, DAVID, son of William Kerr, [1745-1777] a writer and Provost of Forfar, a Major General with 37 years of service in the Cornwall Militia, died 1805. [Montego Bay gravestone, Jamaica]

KERR, DAVID, in Jamaica, cousin and heir of James Ballingall a merchant in Dundee, in 1807, also heir to his cousin John Ballingall of Denoon, a writer in Dundee, who died in 1788. [NRS.S/H]

KERR, THOMAS, late carpenter on HMS Southampton, residing in Forfar, testament, 1794, Comm. St Andrews. [NRS]

KERR, THOMAS, a farmer and cattle dealer in Inverkeiller in 1845. [NRS.CS280.7.8]

KETTLE, MARY, born 1824 in Dundee, emigrated to Prince Edward Island in 1842, died there in 1918. [SPI.99]

KEY, ANDREW, from Carmylie, graduated MA from King's College, Aberdeen, in March 1836. [KCA]

KEY, PETER, born 1761, a shipmaster in Arbroath, died in 1813, husband of Jean Hackney. [Arbroath Abbey gravestone]

KIDD, ALEXANDER, born 174, a shipmaster in Dundee, died 1826, husband of Helen Guild, born 1746, died 1790. [Howff gravestone, Dundee]

KIDD, DAVID, the apprentice Town Clerk of Dundee in 1799. [DCA.B19.3.27/202]

KYD, GEORGE, a weaver, was admitted as a burgess of Arbroath in 1797. [AA.18.941]

KIDD, GEORGE, master of the Belona of Dundee trading between Riga, Latvia, and Dundee in 1818. [NRS.E504.11.21]

KYDD, JAMES, born 1830, son of John Kydd and his wife Helen Dick, died in Castlemaine, Australia, on 18 December 1860. [Carmyllie gravestone]

KIDD, JOHN, a shipmaster in Dundee, testament, 1796, Comm. Brechin. [NRS]

KYD, JOHN, son of George Kyd, a weaver in Dundee, settled in Washington, D.C., before 1831. [NRS.S/H.1851]

KIDD, MARGARET, wife of William Kidd in South Muir, Forfar, , a victim of a mob and rioters in the New Hall, Bell Street, Dundee, in 1842. [NRS.AD14.42.354; JC26.1843.443]

KIDD, ROBERT, a shipmaster in Montrose, testament, 1794, Comm. Brechin. [NRS]

KIDD, ROBERT, a skipper at the Fishmarket, Dundee, master of the Albion of Dundee in 1809, [PAPEI.RG9][Quebec Gazette, 6.7.1809]; master of the Glasgow of Dundee in 1815-1816, [DPCA.655], of the Aid of Dundee trading between Riga and Dundee in 1818, [NRS.E04.11.21], and of the Ocean of Dundee in 1825. [DSR]; master of the brigantine Ocean of Dundee bound from Dundee to Rio de Janeiro on 14 May 1823. [NRS.E504.11.23]

KYD, WILLIAM ANDERSON, born on 23 April 1841 in Dundee, son of David Kyd and his wife Margaret Anderson, was educated at the University of St Andrews in 1867, a minister in New Zealand from 1893, died in Dundee in 1916. [F.7.604]

KIDDIE, ALEXANDER, a skipper in Overgait, Dundee, master of the Thistle in 1818. [DD]

KIDDIE, GEORGE SMALL, born 19 March 1828 in Dundee, married Ann Graham Patterson Clink in Dundee in 1860, emigrated to British Columbia by 1864, settled in Washington Territory in 1868, died in Port Madison there on 29 July 1875. [WSP]

KINCAID, JOHN, a skipper in Fish Street, Dundee, master of the Gipsy of Dundee in 1818, 1824. [DD][DSR]; trading between Leith and Dundee in 1819. [NRS.NRS.E504.24.21]

KING, DAVID, son of Reverend John King in Montrose, a student at Marischal College, Aberdeen, in 1820s, [MCA]

KING, JOHN, an innkeeper in Arbroath, father of John Robert King who settled in Jasper City, Iowa, before 1872. [NRS.S/H]

KINGSTON, JOHN, line manager aboard the Princess Charlotte of Dundee bound for the Davis Strait in 1824. [NRS.E508.129.8]

KINLOCH, ANN, daughter of Sir James Kinloch of Nevoy, testament, 1792, Comm. Brechin. [NRS]

KINLOCH, GEORGE, of Kinloch, Angus, was accused of sedition in 1820. [NRS.AD14.20.178]

KINNEAR, JOHN, born 1775, died 21 December 1842, husband of Ann Bowman, born 1787, died 22 February 1857. [Lochlee gravestone]

KINNEAR, ROBERT, a shipmaster in Dundee, testament, 1799, Comm. Brechin. [NRS]

KINNEAR, WILLIAM, born 1766, a skipper at the Craig, Dundee, in 1809, master of the Isabella of Dundee in 1796, [NRS.CE70.1.8/4]; and of the Hope of Dundee in 1809, [DD], died in 1833. [St Aidan's gravestone, Broughty Ferry]

KIRKCALDY, DAVID, a merchant in Dundee and master of the Hospital there in 1798. [DCA.B19.3.27/1]

KIRKLAND, GEORGE, from Forfar, graduated MA from King's College, Aberdeen, in March 1818. [KCA]

KIRKLAND, WILLIAM, born 1752, a veterinary surgeon in Dundee, died 1787, husband of Jean Smith, born 1753, did 1805. [Howff gravestone, Dundee]

KNIGHT, JOHN, born 1793, son of David Knight and his wife Mary Jamieson, died in Strathalbyn, South Australia, in 1873. [Arbroath Abbey gravestone]

KNIGHT, WALTER, a sailor aboard the Friendship of Dundee at the Davis Straits in 1824. [NRS.E508.130.8]

KNIGHT, WILLIAM, a sawyer, was admitted as a burgess of Arbroath in 1799. [AA.18.941]

LAING, JAMES, from Menmuir, graduated MA from King's College, Aberdeen, in March 1837. [KCA]

LAING, WILLIAM, son of Robert Laing in Logie Pert, a student in Marischal College in 1790s. [MCA]

LAING, JOHN, line manager aboard the Dorothy of Dundee bound for the Davis Straits in 1825. [NRS.E508.130.8]

LAIRD, DAVID, born 1739, a burgess of Dundee in 1783, a Captain, later Rear Admiral of the Royal Navy, died 1815. [Strathmartine gravestone]; inventory, 1815, [NRS.CC20.7.182]

LAIRD, DOUGLAS, sailor aboard the Princess Charlotte of Dundee, bound for the Davis Strait in 1824. [NRS.E508.129.8]

LAIRD, WILLIAM, born 1792, an engineman of the Dundee and Newtyle Railway Company, in Mayfield, Mains and Strathmartine parish, was accused of culpable homicide in 1833. [NRS.AD14.33.65]

LAMB, DAVID, from Brechin, married Miss Brydon, in Montrose on 22 December 1825. [SM.97.126]

LAMB, ELIZABETH, spouse of Colin Alison a writer in Montrose, died there on 29 May 1820. [SM.86.190]

LAMB, JAMES, line manager aboard the Estridge of Dundee, bound for the Davis Straits in 1824. [NRS.E508.129.8]

LAMB, JAMES, a manufacturer in Bucklemaker Wynd, Dundee, victim of an armed robbery in 1840. [NRS.AD14.40.295]

LAMOND, HENDRY WILLIAM, born in Braeminzion, Cortachy, died in the Fitzroy River, Queensland, Australia, on 17 August 1870. [Auchterhouse gravestone]

L'AMY.JAMES, of Dunkenny, the younger, married Mary Carson, second daughter of Dr John Carson a physician in Philadelphia, and widow of William Carson O'Hare in Pittsburg, Pennsylvania, in Edinburgh on 5 November 1811. [SM.73.877]

LANCEMAN, DAVID, a skipper on the Shore, Dundee, in 1782, and in Tyndall's Wynd, Dundee, in 1809, master of the Friendship in 1774, of the Peggy of Dundee in1797, also the Isabel and Pegy of Dundee in 1797, [NRS.CE70.1.8/77]

LANGLANDS, PETER, line manager aboard the Estridge of Dundee, bound for the Davis Straits in 1824. [NRS.E508.129.8]

LANGLANDS, WILLIAM, a merchant in Dundee, son of John Langlands, [1751-1838], and his wife Christian Thoms, [1771-1850], died in Melbourne, Australia, on 21 January 18....., aged 79. [Constitution Road gravestone, Dundee]

LAUCHLAN, JAMES, heir of Thomas Ferrier, late yarn inspector in Kirriemuir, a petition, 1827. [NRS.GD16.41.1078]

LAURENSON, GEORGE SIMSON, born 18 February 1803 in Kinnettles, son of John Laurenson and his wife Margaret Simson, a Brevet Colonel of the Bengal Artillery, died in Cape Town, South Africa, on 26 June 1856. [BA.3.29]

LAW, JAMES, born 1810 in Dundee, died in India on 20 March 1845. [Scotch Burial Ground, Calcutta]

LAW, JOSEPH, steersman of the Friendship of Dundee at the Davis Straits in 1824. [NRS.E508.130.8]

LAWRIE, WILLIAM, from Angus, graduated MA from King's College, Aberdeen, in March 1825. [KCA]

LAWSON, CHARLES, born 1812, son of James Lawson and his wife Elizabeth Smart, died in Craigie, New South Wales, Australia, on 6 April 1875. [Constitution Road gravestone, Dundee]

LAWSON, JAMES, born 1743, died 1792, husband of Margaret Milne, born 1741, died 1792. [Howff gravestone, Dundee]

LAWSON, JAMES, son of Peter Lawson a farmer in Panbride, a student at Marischal College, Aberdeen, in 1830s. [MCA]

LAWSON, PETER, master of the Defiance of Dundee and of the Bridport Packet of Dundee in 1824, also the Osnaburgh of Dundee in 1825, [DSR], and the Atlantic in 1827-1828. [NARA.mf237]

LAWSON, WILLIAM, born 1808 in Dundee, a merchant in New York, died in Brooklyn, N.Y., on 15 October 1852. [ANY]

LECKIE, DAVID, born 1807 in Forfar, an accountant in Charleston, South Carolina, was naturalised there on 12 July 1843. [NARA.M1183.1]

LEES, ALEXANDER, master of the Alexander of Dundee trading between St Petersburg, Russia, and Dundee in 1819. [NRS.E504.11.21]

LEIGHTON, DAVID, in Tannadice, testament, 1799, Comm. St Andrews. [NRS]

LEIGHTON, JAMES, from Forfar, settled in Kingston, Jamaica, died aboard the RMS Orinocco on 24 November 1852. [W.1394]

LEIGHTON, ROBERT, a merchant in Montrose, testament, 1795, Comm. Brechin. [NRS]

LESLIE, EDWARD, born in Dundee, a publisher and bookseller there, a merchant who died in Dundas, Halton County, Upper Canada, on 16 August 1829. [DPCA.1379]

LESLIE, PETER, born 1820, died Inland, Adams County, Nebraska, on 12 July 1872. [Arbroath Abbey gravestone]

LEUCHARS, ALEXANDER, born 1777, feuar of Scouringburn, Dundee, died 18 May 1857, husband of Margaret Barrie, born 1796, died 18 December 1879. [Balgay gravestone, Dundee]

LEY, JOHN, schoolmaster in Monifieth, a letter to Alexander Nicoll in 1820. [NRS.GD16.46.82]

LIGHTON, GEORGE, a merchant, was admitted as a burgess of Arbroath in 1795. [AA.18.941]

LIGHTON, JAMES, a burgess and guilds-brother of Arbroath, husband of Margaret Vannet, 1796. [Arbroath Abbey gravestone]

LIGHTON, JOHN, in Dunninald, was admitted as a burgess of Arbroath in 1792. [AA.18.941]

LILLIE, Reverend JAMES, born 1800 in Montrose, died in Kansas City, Missouri, on 7 October 1875. [EC.2840]

LINDSAY, ELIZABETH, in Brechin Road, Arbroath, a victim of theft in 1845. [NRS.JC26.1845.418]

LINDSAY, JAMES BOWMAN, born 8 September 1799 in Carmyllie, who was educated at the University of St Andrews, an inventor, died in Dundee on 29 June 1862. [Western gravestone, Dundee]

LINDSAY, JAMES, born 1815, son of Robert Lindsay, [1783-1864]; and his wife Jean Lindsay, [1788-1852], died in New York on 18 August 1848. [Kirriemuir gravestone]

LINDSAY, JOHN, a shoemaker, was admitted as a burgess of Arbroath in 1797. [AA.18.941]

LINDSAY, ROBERT, born 14 April 1810, died at North Tarry on 22 September 1876, husband of Agnes Muir, born 1822, died 1853. [St Vigeans gravestone]

LITHGOW, AARON, a skipper in Seagait, Dundee, master of the Norval of Dundee in 1809, [DD], of the Venerable in 1816-1818, of the Rosina from 1822 to 1825. [NARA.m575/2] [DPCA.755/1214][DD]

LITHGOW, ROBERT, master of the Concord of Dundee in 1809. [DD]

LITTLEJOHN, ALEXANDER, a tailor, was admitted as a burgess of Arbroath in 1790. [AA.18.941]

LITTLEJOHN, ALEXANDER, a weaver, was admitted as a burgess of Arbroath in 1797. [AA.18.941]

LITTLEJOHN, JAMES, a flaxdresser, was admitted as a burgess of Arbroath in 1797. [AA.18.941]

LITTLEJOHN, JAMES, born 1812, a weaver in Blackhouse Wynd, Abbeylands, Arbroath, was accused of theft from the Spinning Mill in Lindsay Street, Arbroath, in 1829. [NRS.AD14.29.117]GD45.16.2066]

LITTLEJOHN, WILLIAM, a shoemaker, was admitted as a burgess of Arbroath in 1797. [AA.18.941]

LIVINGSTONE, DAVID, a writer in Dundee in 1799. [DCA.B19.3.27/253]

LOCKHART, PETER, in Broughty Ferry, a tack in the Links of Barnhill in 1839. [NRS]

LORIMER, DAVID, harpooner aboard the Estridge of Dundee, bound for the Davis Straits in 1824. [NRS.E508.129.8]

LOUSON, DAVID R., from Angus, graduated MA from King's College, Aberdeen, in March 1823. [KCA]

LOUSON, JOHN, a weaver in Carnoustie, a tack, 1840. [NRS.GD45.16]

LOUSON, WILLIAM, a wright in Carnoustie, a tack, 1840. [NRS.GD45.16]

LOWE, CATHERINE, daughter of Dr Joseph Lowe a physician in Unthank by Brechin, versus her husband William Allardyce, formerly of the Honourable East India Company Service, now a Captain of the Angus Regiment of Fencibles, a Process of Divorce in 1802. [NRS.CC8.6.1121]

LOW, Reverend James, in Miramachi, New Brunswick, son and heir of James Low a slater in Dundee, 1816. [NRS.S/H]

LOW, JAMES, from Forfar, graduated MA from King's College, Aberdeen, in March 1826, later a minister in Victoria, Australia. [KCA]

LOW, JOHN, a hardware merchant at the Cross of Forfar, a victim of theft in 1825. [NRS.AD14.25.244]

LOW, JOHN, born 1820, son of Joseph Low and his wife Magdalene Hovell, died in Calcutta, India, on 5 September 1841. [Constitution Road gravestone, Dundee]

LOW, MARGARET DUN, fourth daughter of Robert Low the cashier of the Dundee Banking Company, married Robert Eglinton, a merchant, in Calcutta, India, on 1 August 1825. [SM.97.254]

LOW, ROBERT, a merchant in Dundee in 1791. [DCA.B19.3.27/262]

LOW, WILLIAM, born 1750, died 1812, husband of Janet Glenday, born 1756, died 1802. [Howff gravestone, Dundee]

LOW, WILLIAM, a machine maker in Monifieth, 1843. [NRS.GD280.5.24]

LOWDEN, DAVID, born 1739, died 1811. [Howff gravestone, Dundee]

LOWDEN, GILBERT, a carter in Hilltown, Dundee, in 1792. [DCA.B19.3.27/1/12]

LOWDEN, HENRY, born 1828, son of Alexander Lowden and his wife Christian Ramsay, died in Australia on 25 November 1867. [Strathmartine gravestone]

LOWNIE, WILLIAM, aboard the Princess Charlotte of Dundee bound for the Davis Strait in 1824. [NRS.E508.129.8]

LOWSON, ANN BANNERMAN, daughter of George Lowson and his wife Catherine Paton, died in Plymouth, New Zealand, on 23 November 1860. [Fowlis Easter gravestone]

LOWSON, JAMES, a wheelwright in Westhaven, and family, emigrated via Dundee aboard the Providence of Perth, master Robert Nicoll, bound for New York in May 1819. [NRS.CE70.1.5]

LUCKIE, ALEXANDER, born 1771, son of William Luckie and his wife Isabel Chalmers, died aboard HMS Valiant in Port Royal, Jamaica, on 2 July 1799. [Howff gravestone, Dundee]

LUKE, JOHN, a merchant in Dundee, trustee of David Keir in St James, Jamaica, in 1814. [NRS.RD5.71.472]

LUNAN, ALEXANDER, of Bishoploch and Linthill, born 1783, died 28 October 1847. [St Vigeans gravestone]

LUNAN, DAVID, a former student at the University of St Andrews, son of John Lunan a tenant in Wester Keith, Lundie, was accused of robbery in 1821. [NRS.AD14.21.36]

LUNAN, JOHN, in North Mains, Kinnettles, was accused of theft in 1825. [NRS.AD14.25.244]

LUNAN, ROBERT, born 1750, proprietor of Linthill and Bishoploch, died 12 July 1838, husband of Elisabeth Bell, born 1750, died 24 June 1836. [St Vigeans gravestone]

LUNDIE, MARY, born 1841, daughter of Andrew Lundie and his wife Jane Ruxton, died in Denver, Colorado, on 30 July 1885. [Arbroath Abbey gravestone]

LYELL, CHARLES, was admitted as a burgess of Arbroath in 1793. [AA.18.941]

LYELL, CHARLES, of Kinnordy, Fellow of the Royal Society, was granted a Doctor of Laws degree by Marischal College, Aberdeen, in 1843. [MCA]

LYALL, JAMES GIBSON, in Jamaica, nephew and heir of David Lyall of Gallery in 1816, [NRS.S/H]; late in Jamaica, son of James Gibson Lyall, was granted the lands of Gallery on 1 June 1816. [NRS.RGS.154.17]

LYELL, JAMES, a skipper in King Street, Dundee, [DD]; master of the Active in 1818, of the Unity of Dundee in 1825, [DSR], and of the 200 ton brig Leda in 1828. [DPCA.1345]

LYALL, JAMES, sailor aboard the Princess Charlotte of Dundee bound for the Davis Strait in 1824. [NRS.E508.129.8]

LYALL, JAMES, in Old Downie farm, Monikie, was a victim of housebreaking in 1829. [NRS.AD14.29.166]

LYALL, JOHN, born 1836, died in St Croix, Danish West Indies, on 18 March 1856. [Howff gravestone, Dundee]

LYALL, THOMAS, of Gardyne, testament, 1793, Comm. St Andrews. [NRS]

LYON, DAVID, a merchant in London in 1799, son of John Lyon of Kinnaird a merchant in Dundee. [DCA.B19.3.27/239]

LYON, GEORGE, of Wester Ogil, Forfar, a student in Marischal College around 1800, later a Writer to the Signet. [MCA]

LYON, HUGH, a Captain in the Service of the East India Company, testament, 1800. [NRS]

LYON, JOHN, 'a botanist who travelled the Southern wilds of North America', died in Nashville, North Carolina [sic], on 14 August 1814. [Dundee gravestone]

LYON, WILLIAM, son of Reverend James Lyon in Glamis, graduated MA from Marischal College, Aberdeen, in 1816, later a minister in Aberdeen. [MCA]

MCARTHUR, JAMES, in Monikie, sequestration, 1848. [NRS.CS279.1912]

MCBAIN, JAMES, surgeon aboard the Estridge of Dundee, bound for the Davis Straits in 1824. [NRS.E508.129.8]

MACBETH, JAMES, born 1805, a cooper who emigrated from Dundee on the brig Sprightly to Charleston, South Carolina, in 1828. [NARA]

MCCOMIE, THOMAS, born 1750, a weaver in Hawkhill, Dundee, died 1790. [Howff gravestone, Dundee]

MCCONACHIE. GEORGE, son of George McConachie a schoolmaster in Logie Pert, graduated MA from Marischal College, Aberdeen, in 1823. [MCA]

MCCULLOCH, JOHN, born 1800, a merchant who emigrated via Dundee on the barque Herald bound for Charleston, South Carolina, landed there in October 1826. [NARA]

MCDONALD, DONALD, married, a labourer in Kirkinch, parish of Eassie and Nevay, was accused of bigamy in 1839. [NRS.AD14.39.64]

MCDONALD, JAMES, a weaver, was admitted as a burgess of Arbroath in 1797. [AA.18.941]

MCDONALD, JAMES, master of the Hunter of Dundee, in 1824. [DSR]; testament, 1836, [NRS.SC45.31.3.40]

MCDONALD, JOHN, a mason, was admitted as a burgess of Arbroath in 1798. [AA.18.941]

MCDONNELL, JAMES, born 1802, a baker who emigrated from Dundee on the brig Comely of Dundee bound for Charleston, South Carolina, landed there on 17 October 1820. [NRS.E504.11.21][NARA]

MCEWAN, DAVID, born 1796, of George Square, Dundee, was accused of robbing, rioting and assaulting army officers at Dudhope Barracks, Dundee, in 1832. [NRS.AD14.32.29]

MCEWAN, GEORGE, son of David McEwan in St Cyr, Grenada, died in Montrose on 14 November 1823. [SM.92.768]

MCEWAN, JAMES, born 1750, minister of the Associated Anti-Burgher Congregation of Dundee, died 1813. [Howff gravestone, Dundee]

MCEWAN, MARY, was found guilty of child murder in Balzeodie, Menmuir, was sentenced to transportation to the colonies for 7 years, in 1841. [NRS.JC26.1841.402]

MCFARLANE, FREDERICK, a minister in Montrose from 1787 to 1795, then settled on Long Island, USA. [UPC.1.6]

MCGHIE, JOHN, an Excise officer, was admitted as a burgess of Arbroath in 1794. [AA.18.941]

MCGRANE, MICHAEL, in Bordeaux, France, was admitted as a burgess of Arbroath in 1791. [AA.18.941]

MCGREGOR, DUNCAN, a labourer in Kidd Street, Arbroath, was accused of bigamy in 1844. [NRS.AD14.44.70]

MCGREGOR, JOHN, a journeyman shoemaker in Bucklemaker Wynd, Dundee, was accused of membership of an unlawful combination in 1820. [NRS.AD14.20.215]

MCGROUTHER, GEORGE, sailor aboard the Princess Charlotte of Dundee bound for the Davis Strait in 1824. [NRS.E508.129.8]

MCINTOSH, GEORGE, a wright, was admitted as a burgess of Arbroath in 1797. [AA.18.941]

MCINTOSH, ISABEL, servant to William Lindsay a merchant in Dundee, testament, 1796, Comm. Brechin. [NRS]

MCINTOSH, JOHN, a bookbinder, was admitted as a burgess of Arbroath in 1797. [AA.18.941]

MCINTOSH, THOMAS, master of the <u>Psyche of Dundee</u> 1821-1822. [NARA.mf237]

MCKAY, DONALD, a mason, was admitted as a burgess of Arbroath in 1798. [AA.18.941]

MACKAY, JOHN, born 1807, a weaver in Arbroath, a court witness in 1824. [NRS.AD14.24.110]

MCKENZIE, ALEXANDER, a merchant in Dundee, testament, 1800, Comm. Brechin. [NRS]

MCKENZIE, KENNETH, born 1808, a painter, son of Thomas McKenzie a shoemaker in Nethergait, Dundee, was accused of robbing, rioting and assaulting army officers at Dudhope Barracks, Dundee, in 1832. [NRS.AD14.32.29]

MCKENZIE, ROBINSON, born 1814, a shoemaker in Pierhead, Kirriemuir, lawful husband of Isabella Fraser in Arbroath, was accused of bigamously marrying Margaret Petrie in Cononsyth, Carmyllie, 1836. [NRS.AD14.36.74]

MCKENZIE, WILLIAM, a journeyman shoemaker in Fish Street, Dundee, was accused of membership of an unlawful combination in 1820. [NRS.AD14.20.215]

MCKENZIE, WILLIAM, from Angus, graduated MA from King's College, Aberdeen, in March 1823. [KCA]

MCKENZIE, WILLIAM LYON, born 1794 in Dundee, emigrated to Canada in 1825, a political radical, died in Toronto, Ontario, on 28 August 1861. [GM.NS2/11.567]

MACKIE, JAMES, a fresh or green man aboard the <u>Friendship of Dundee</u> at the Davis Straits in 1824. [NRS.E508.130.8]

MACKIE, JAMES, [1], harpooner aboard the <u>Princess Charlotte of Dundee</u> bound for the Davis Strait in 1824. [NRS.E508.129.8]

MACKIE, JAMES, [2], line manager aboard the Princess Charlotte of Dundee bound for the Davis Strait in 1824. [NRS.E508.129.8]

MCKINLAY, ALEXANDER, a merchant in Brechin, 1846. [NRS.CS313.568]

MCKRABIE, JAMES, a merchant in Ethie, Inverkeilor, testament, 1799, Comm. St Andrews. [NRS]

MCLACHLAN, JAMES, line manager aboard the Dorothy of Dundee bound for the Davis Straits in 1825. [NRS.E508.130.8]

MCLAUCHLAN, WILLIAM, line manager aboard the Estridge of Dundee, bound for the Davis Straits in 1824. [NRS.E508.129.8]

MCLACHLAN, WILLIAM, son of William McLachlan, a seaman in Dundee, and his wife Isabel Elder, [1792-1857], settled in Melbourne, Australia. [Longforgan gravestone]

MCLEAN, DUNCAN, born 1749, a merchant in Petersburg, Virginia, died there on 10 April 1814, husband of Janet Miln in Dundee. [Howff gravestone, Dundee]

MCLEISH, JOHN, a merchant in Brechin, sederunt books, 1810-1811. [NRS.CS96.3359]

MCLEOD, JOHN, a bleacher of Turnbull and Company at Claverhouse bleachfield, Trottick, parish of Mains and Strathmartine, was accused of assaulting officers of the law in 1837. [NRS.AD14.37.122]

MCMILLAN, JANE, a hawker of stoneware, in Montrose, was accused of mobbing and rioting there in 1813. [NRS.AD14.13.84]

MCMORAN, JANE, born 1778, with Robert McMoran born 1820, emigrated via Dundee aboard the brig Rosina bound for South Carolina, landed in Charleston, S.C., in February 1823. [NARA]

MCNAB, JOHN, a thief imprisoned in Brechin Tolbooth, found guilty and sentenced to six months imprisonment, 1827. [NRS.JC26.1827.16]

MCNICOLL, JAMES, factor for the Earl of Airlie, a deed of factory in 1810; a disposition, 1830. [NRS.GD16.41.1028; GD16.13.109/111]

MCNICOLL, JOHN, at Craig, a letter to William Blackadder in Glamis, 1837. [NRS.GD16.39.31]

MCNICOL, PETER, a farm servant in Tulloes, Dunnichen, was accused of theft in 1834. [NRS.AD14.34.335]

MCPHERSON, ALEXANDER, harpooner aboard the <u>Dorothy of Dundee</u> bound for the Davis Straits in 1825. [NRS.E508.130.8]

MCPHERSON, ALEXANDER, in Shore Wynd, Montrose, a victim of a housebreaker in 1830. [NRS.AD14.30.68]

MCPHERSON, ROBERT, from Forfar, graduated MA from King's College, Aberdeen, on 31 March 1827. [KCA]

MCQUEEN, HUGH, a tenant in Careston, in 1834. [NRS.CS.46.1833.174]

MCTAGGART, DAVID, from Angus, graduated MA from King's College, Aberdeen, on 31 March 1827, later a minister. [KCA]

MCWATTIE, ISOBEL, a weaver in Sparrowcroft, Forfar, a victim of theft in 1825. [NRS.AD14.25.244]

MACHAR, JOHN, from Angus, graduated MA from King's College, Aberdeen, on 25 March 1814, later was a minister in Kingston, Canada. [KCA]

MAIDEN, WILLIAM, a merchant in Dundee, testament, 1796, Comm. Brechin. [NRS]

MAIRS, ALEXANDER, a dyer, was admitted as a burgess of Arbroath in 1797. [AA.18.941]

MAIR, DAVID, from Kirriemuir, graduated MA from King's College, Aberdeen, in March 1850, later a United Presbyterian minister in Killaig, Ireland. [KCA]

MAITLAND, or PYOTT, JAMES, son of James Pyott a merchant in Montrose, a merchant in New York, a deed, 1797. [NRS.RD4.263.1084]

MALCOLM, CARNEGIE, a journeyman shoemaker in Overgait, Dundee, was accused of membership of an unlawful combination in 1820. [NRS.AD14.20.215]

MALCOLM, ROBERT DOIG, born 1843, son of David Malcolm and his wife Elspeth Doig, died in Belle Fourche, South Dakota, in 1909. [Glamis gravestone]

MANN, ALEXANDER, a weaver, was admitted as a burgess of Arbroath in 1797. [AA.18.941]

MANN, JOHN, born 1771, a weaver and pendicler in Downie Muir, was buried in Kirkbuddo on 24 April 1849. [Monikie Burial Register]

MANN. WILLIAM, from Angus, graduated MA from King's College, Aberdeen, on 27 March 1800. [KCA]

MARNIE, DAVID, a shoemaker in Arbroath by 1766, a burgess there in 1791. [Arbroath Examination Roll][AA.18.941]

MARNIE, JAMES, born 1776, a manufacturer and merchant in Millgate, Arbroath, 1817, Provost of Arbroath, died 12 March 1849, husband of Mary Auchterlony, born 1773, died 1856. [NRS.CS96.405] [Arbroath Abbey gravestone]; he exported a cargo of linen from Dundee aboard the Peace, Captain Bruce, bound for New York in September 1820. [NRS.E504.11.21]

MARR, JOHN, line manager of the Friendship of Dundee at the Davis Straits in 1824. [NRS.E508.130.8]

MARSHALL, ALEXANDER, born 1795, a surgeon from Dundee, was drowned in the wreck of the whaling ship Oscar of Aberdeen in 1813.

MARSHALL, THOMAS, was accused of the murder of John Allan at the Mill of Dun, Burnside of Wedderburn, Murroes, in 1824, found guilty and was transported to the colonies for 14 years. [NRS.JC26.1824.92]

MARSHALL, WILLIAM, a merchant in Dundee in 1799. [DCA.B19.3.27/159]

MARSHALL, WILLIAM, a merchant in Dundee, and his wife Christian Pilmore, were parents of William Marshall, born 1740, who died in New Orleans, Louisiana, on 23 December 1803. [Howff, Dundee]

MARTIN, ALEXANDER, born 29 February 1796 in Forfar, a stone cutter who emigrated via Halifax, Nova Scotia, to New York where he was naturalised on 2 May 1829. [NARA]

MARTIN, ALEXANDER, a skipper in Couttie's Wynd, Dundee, master of the Fleece in 1818, trading between Riga, Latvia, and Dundee in 1818. [NRS.E504.11.21] [DD]

MARTIN, ALEXANDER, a labourer at Brae of Pert, Logie Pert, was accused of bigamy in 1842. [NRS.AD14.42.150]

MARTIN, CHARLES, at the Mill of Ravernie, Lintrathen, testament, 1796, Comm. St Andrews. [NRS]

MARTIN, JAMES, a book-seller in Dundee in 1799. [DCA.B19.3.27/266]

MARTIN, JAMES, son of John Martin a farmer in Brechin, graduated MA from Marischal College in 1816, later a minister. [MCA]

MARTIN, JEAN, in Hawkhill, Dundee, daughter of James Martin a tenant in Bullion, testament, 1796, Comm. Brechin. [NRS]

MARTIN, PATRICK, in Hawkhill, Dundee, husband of Janet Bower born 1751, died 1811. [Howff gravestone, Dundee]

MARTIN, Lieutenant ROBERT, was admitted as a burgess of Arbroath in 1795. [AA.18.941]

MARTIN, WILLIAM, a skipper in the Murraygait, Dundee, master of the Alexander of Dundee from 1817 to 1821, [DD][NRS.E504.15.114; E504.11.21/22]; of the Clio in 1818, [DD]; and of the Nancy of Dundee son of, born 29 February 1796 in Forfar, a stonecutter who emigrated via Halifax, Nova Scotia, to New York City, naturalised there on 2 May 1829. [NARA]

MASTERTON, WILLIAM, married Elizabeth Machir in Dunnichen in 1813, Ann Walker in Aberdeen in 1821, and Catherine Burnett in Mid

Wynd, Dundee, in 1836, was accused of bigamy in 1837, trial papers. [NRS.JC26.1837.447]

MATHER, DAVID, a weaver in Brechin, testament, 1800, Comm. Brechin. [NRS]

MATHER, DAVID, and Margaret Easton, both from Forfar, were married in St John, New Brunswick, on 14 May 1820. [CG.17.5.1820]

MATHER, ROBERT, a tanner in Dundee, sequestration in 1826. [SM.97.253]

MATHERS, SAMUEL, born 1735, a butcher in Dundee, died 1812, husband of Christian Murdoch born 1733, died 1818. [Howff gravestone, Dundee]

MATTHEW, ANDREW, a weaver, was admitted as a burgess of Arbroath in 1797. [AA.18.941]

MATTHEW, GEORGE, born 1740, a maltman in Dundee, died 1801, husband of Janet Wood, born 1748, died 1796. [Howff gravestone, Dundee]

MATHEW, DAVID, in Liff and Benvie parish, was murdered in 1822. [NRS.AD14.33.65]

MATTHEW, JAMES, the younger, a manufacturer in Dundee in 1799, son of James Matthew the elder and his wife Isobel Flowers, daughter of James Flowers a manufacturer in Dundee. [DCA.B19.3.27/215]

MATTHEW, THOMAS, from Dundee, emigrated via Belfast, Ireland, to New York on the George, landed there on 14 October 1815. [NWI]

MATTHEW, WALTER, was admitted as a burgess of Arbroath in 1797. [AA.18.941]

MATTHEW, WILLIAM, son of John Matthew and his wife Barbara Moir, died in New Zealand in 1862. [Eastern Necropolis, Dundee]

MATTHEWSON, JOHN, born 1831, son of John Matthewson and his wife Jessie Isles, died in Newcastle, New South Wales, Australia, on 2 February 1884. [Arbroath Abbey gravestone]

MATTHEWSON, ROBERT, born 1729, a manufacturer in Dundee, died in 1802. [Howff gravestone, Dundee]

MATTERS, JOHN, a flax dresser in the West Port, Dundee, versus David Millar, a brewer in Hawkhill, Dundee, 1807. [NRS.CS271.447]

MAUER, ELISABETH, born 1749, died 1798, wife of John Tod a baker in Dundee. [Howff gravestone, Dundee]

MAULE, WILLIAM, of Panmure, versus David Traill in Panbride, in 1810. [NRS.CS271.53825]; Master Mason of Dundee, Masonic certificates, 1815. [NRS.GD45.15.97]

MAULE, WILLIAM, of Fearn, a letter, 1847. [NRS.GD45.14,894]

MAVOR, ROBERT, a skipper in Tindall's Wynd, Dundee, in 1818, [DD]; master of the Barbara of Dundee, trading between Riga, Latvia, and Dundee in 1819, [NRS.E504.11.21]; and of the Midas of Dundee, a brig, in 1824. [DSR][DPCA.1138/1203/1230]

MAXWELL, DAVID, of Balmyle, an advocate, testaments, 1795-1796, Comm. Brechin. [NRS]

MAXWELL, GEORGE, of Balmyle, former Provost of Dundee, testament, 1796, Comm. Brechin. [NRS]

MAXWELL, JOHN, late in Jamaica, son of William Maxwell, was admitted as a burgess of Dundee on 4 February 1818. [DBR]

MAXWELL, PATRICK, Customs Controller in Dundee, testament, 1797, Comm. Brechin. [NRS]

MAXWELL, WILLIAM, a sailor aboard the Friendship of Dundee at the Davis Straits in 1824. [NRS.E508.130.8]

MAXWELL, WILLIAM, son of David Maxwell a farmer in Dunnichen, a student at Marischal College, Aberdeen, in 1840s, late Free Church minister at Deerness. [MCA]

MEAL, JOHN, a wright in Dundee, versus John Thom, a shoemaker in Dundee, 1811. [NRS.CS36.2.49]

MEALMAKER, GEORGE, sailor aboard the Estridge of Dundee, bound for the Davis Straits in 1824. [NRS.E508.129.8]

MEALMAKER, JOHN, a fresh or green man aboard the Estridge of Dundee bound for the Davis Straits in 1824. [NRS.E508.129.8]

MEARNS, ANDREW, born 1731, a mariner in Montrose in 1769, master of the Jean of Montrose, died in 1815, husband of Margaret Law who died in 1800. [Montrose gravestone] [NRS.CE70.1.8/60]

MEARNS, ANDREW, born 1784, son of William Mearns, died at sea in 1806. [Montrose gravestone]

MEARNS, JOHN, master of the Lovely Betty of Dundee and of the Shields Packet of Dundee in 1795, [NRS.CE70.1.8/5, 12, 58], and of the Clio of Dundee in 1824. [DSR]; master of the Urania of Dundee was shipwrecked when bound from St Petersburg, Russia, to Greenock, Scotland, in November 1834. [MD.125]

MEARNS, WILLIAM, born 1756, a shipmaster who died at sea in 1806. [Montrose gravestone]

MEDLEY, Mrs BESS, and her daughter Fanny, at Holden Hall, Muirdrum, letters, 1840. [NRS.GD139.474]

MEEK, DAVID, born 1806, died 19 July 1862, husband of Janet Dick born 1809, died 6 November 1881. [Barry gravestone]

MELESS, GEORGE, from Perth, was admitted as a merchant burgess of Arbroath in 1790. [AA.18.941]

MELVILLE, DAVID, and his wife Isabel Ross or Grant, were parents of David Hay Melville, born 1857, died in Port Adelaide, South Australia, in June 1902, [Rosehill gravestone, Montrose]

MELVILLE, JAMES WALKER, son of David Melville, [1787-1815], and his wife Elizabeth Tulloch, [1793-1835], a shipwright who died in Germantown, Australia, aged 65. [Howff gravestone, Dundee]

METHVEN, CHARLES CAITHNESS, an agent in Dundee, later in Jamaica, died on 19 April 1845, inventory 1853. [NRS.SC70.1.80]

MICHIE, JEAN, widow of James Duncan of Woodhouse, testament, 1795. Comm. Brechin. [NRS]

MIDDLETON, DAVID, a merchant burgess of Arbroath in 1798. [AA.18.941]

MIDDLETON, DAVID, a carter in the west town end of Forfar, was accused of housebreaking at Balgavies, Aberlemno, in 1830. [NRS.AD14.30.56; JC26.1830.16]

MIDDLETON, JANET, born 1762, wife of Peter Smith, [1772-1810], from Brechin, died in Andover, Massachusetts, in 1839. [Brechin Cathedral gravestone]

MILBURN, WILLIAM OGILVY, from Brechin, died in Kingston, Jamaica, on 18 June 1835. [AJ.4573]

MILL, JAMES, from Carnoustie, son of William Mill, a writer in Arbroath later a merchant at St Ann's Bay, Jamaica, in 1853. [NRS.CS313.38]

MILL, MARGARET, born 1802, a servant of Samuel Renny, a manufacturer and bleacher in Arbroath, was accused of theft from the drying park at the foot of Applegate, Arbroath, in 1825. [NRS.AD14.25.67]

MILLS, DAVID, born 1850, son of James Mills and his wife Isobel Brodie, died in Mansfield, Australia, on 8 July 1883. [Western gravestone, Dundee]

MILLS, JAMES, a skipper at the Fishmarket in Dundee, master of the Active of Dundee in 1795, [NRS.CE70.1.8/5, 37]; master of the Perthshire of Dundee in 1809, of the Defiance of Dundee in 1818, 1824, also the Osnaburgh of Dundee in 1824. [DSR][DD]

MILL, PETER, a sailor of the Friendship of Dundee at the Davis Straits in 1824. [NRS.E508.130.8]

MILL, ROBERT, steersman aboard the Princess Charlotte of Dundee bound for the Davis Strait in 1824. [NRS.E508.129.8]

MILL, WILLIAM, a merchant in Arbroath in 1794. [NRS.CE70.1.8]

MILL, WILLIAM, a fresh or green man aboard the <u>Friendship of Dundee</u> at the Davis Straits in 1824. [NRS.E508.130.8]

MILL, WILLIAM, eldest son of ... Mill of Millfield the Provost of Arbroath, died at St Ann's Bay, Jamaica, on 9 November 1850. [FJ.941][W.1183][EEC.22068]

MILLER, ALEXANDER, a sailor aboard the whaler <u>Mary Ann of Dundee</u> from Dundee to Greenland on 4 March 1813, abandoned the ship on return at Aberdeen to avoid the Press Gang on 16 August 1813. [NRS.E508.115.8]

MILLER, ALEXANDER, an ironmonger from Dundee, later a planter at Fort Niagara, New York, by 1819. [NRS.CS17.1.28/329]

MILLER, CHARLES, born 1732, a manufacturer, died 1812, husband of Christian Blair, born 1736, died 1800. [Howff gravestone, Dundee]

MILLER, DAVID, tenant in the Mains of Glamis in 1801. [NRS.GD45.17.1183]

MILLER, DAVID, born 1808, son of William Miller and his wife Isabella Gilchrist, was drowned in the St Lawrence River, Canada, on 12 June 1827. [Howff gravestone, Dundee]

MILLER, JAMES, a baker burgess of Arbroath in 1799. [AA.18.941]

MILLER, JAMES, born 1787 in Dundee, died in India on 4 May 1829. [Scotch Burial Ground gravestone, Calcutta]

MILLER, JAMES F., son of Thomas Miller, a skipper in Dundee, [died 1803], and his wife Elizabeth Gordon, [died 1818], a shipmaster in New York. [Howff, Dundee, gravestone]

MILLAR, PETER, a sailor aboard the <u>Dorothy of Dundee</u> bound for the Davis Straits in 1825. [NRS.E508.130.8]

MILLER, ROBERT JOHNSTONE, born on 11 July 1758, son of G. and M. Miller in Baldovie, emigrated to America before 1784, an Episcopalian minister in North Carolina, died at John's River, Burke County, on 13 May 1834. [Caldwell County gravestone, N.C.] [Western Carolinian.31.5.1834][History of Rowan County]

MILLER, ROBERT, a tanner and leather-merchant in Brechin, Sederunt books, 1804-1811. [NRS.CS96.4246]

MILLER, ROBERT, born 1817, son of David Miller, [1776-1824], a brewer, and his wife Isabella Gilchrist, [1767-1849], died in New Orleans, Louisiana, on 6 December 1850. [Howff gravestone, Dundee]

MILLER, THOMAS, a manufacturer, was admitted as a burgess of Arbroath in 1794. [AA.18.941]

MILLER, THOMAS, master of the Caledonia of Dundee in 1809, [DD]; a skipper in Dundee, [died 1809], and his wife Elizabeth Gardiner, [died 1818], parents of James F. Miller who settled in New York. [Howff gravestone, Dundee]

MILLER, WILLIAM, born 1781 in Montrose, a baker, was naturalised in Charleston, South Carolina, on 27 May 1807. [NARA.M1183.1]; died on 8 November 1814. [Old Scots gravestone, Charleston]

MILLER, WILLIAM, born 1802, son of David Miller and his wife Isabella Gilchrist, died in Jamaica in 1817. [Howff gravestone, Dundee]

MILLAR, WILLIAM, a quarrier in Charleston, Glamis, accused of assault in 1839. [NRS.AD14.39.129]

MILLS, DAVID, born 1850, son of James Mills and his wife Isobel Brodie, died in Mansfield, Australia, on 8 July 1883. [Dundee Western gravestone]

MILLS, WILLIAM, a merchant in Arbroath in 1794. [NRS.CE70.1.7]

MILNE, ALEXANDER, a currier, was admitted as a burgess of Arbroath in 1797. [AA.18.941]

MILNE, CHARLES, a tailor, was admitted as a burgess of Arbroath in 1791. [AA.18.941]

MILNE, DAVID, born 1735, died in 1822. [Montrose gravestone]

MILNE, DAVID, born 1738, a brewer burgess and guilds-brother of Arbroath, died 1795, husband of Isabel Milne. [Arbroath Abbey gravestone]

MILNE, DAVID, a weaver, was admitted as a burgess of Arbroath in 1797. [AA.18.941]

MILN, DAVID, line manager aboard the <u>Estridge of Dunmaster of Dundee</u> bound for the Davis Straits in 1824. [NRS.E508.129.8]

MILNE, DAVID, from Forfar, graduated MA from King's College, Aberdeen, in March 1832. [KCA]

MILNE, DAVID, formerly in Hillhead of Careston, later in Tigerton of Memus, records, 1841. [NRS.CS97.98.M21]

MILNE, DUNCAN, a weaver, was admitted as a burgess of Arbroath in 1799. [AA.18.941]

MILNE, JAMES, a rope-maker, was admitted as a burgess of Arbroath in 1793. [AA.18.941]

MILNE, JAMES, from Airlie, graduated MA from King's College, Aberdeen, in March 1845. [KCA]

MILNE, JAMES, from Lintrathen, graduated MA from King's College, Aberdeen, in March 1857, later school master at Helston. [KCA]

MILNE, JAMES, born 1746 in Dundee, '40 years in Charleston, South Carolina', died on 27 March 1805. [Bahamas Royal Gazette, 7.5.1805]

MILNE, JOHN, a flax-dresser in Montrose, testament, 1795, Comm. Brechin. [NRS]

MILNE, JOHN, a wright in Dundee, in 1796. [DCA.B19.3.26/1]

MILNE, JOHN, born 1768, in Glen Catt, died 2 September 1818, husband of Susan Farquharson, born 1768, died 2 September 1843. [Lochlee gravestone]

MILNE, JOHN, a wheelwright, was admitted as a burgess of Arbroath in 1797. [AA.18.941]

MILN, JOHN, an innkeeper, was granted a tack in Slateford, Edzell, in 1838. [NRS.GD45.16.1919]

MILNE, JOHN, son of Alexander Milne a shoemaker in Montrose, a student at Marischal College, Aberdeen, in 1836. [MCA]

MILNE, JOHN, from Forfar, graduated MA from King's College, Aberdeen, in March 1849. [KCA]

MILNE, JOHN, of Ravensby and Grange of Barry, born 1833, died 7 February 1916, husband of Eliza Lyall Simpson, born 1831, died 4 November 1905. [Barry gravestone]

MILNE, NICOLSON, from Angus, graduated MA from King's College, Aberdeen, in April 1830. [KCA]

MILNE, PETER, a schoolmaster, was admitted as a burgess of Arbroath in 1791. [AA.18.941]

MILNE, WILLIAM, a haberdasher in Dundee, sederunt book, 1815-1816. [NRS.CS96.392]

MITCHELL, ALEXANDER, son of Reverend James Mitchell in Aberlemno, a student at Marischal College around 1810. [MCA]

MITCHELL, ALEXANDER, a skipper in Tindall's Wynd, Dundee, master of the Archduke of Dundee in 1818, 1825, [DD][DSR]; testament, 1840. [NRS.SC45.31.5.278]

MITCHELL, ALEXANDER, in Chapelshade, Dundee, an officer of the law, was assaulted in Trottick in 1837. [NRS.AD14.37.123]

MITCHELL, ANN, in Dundee, testament, 1793, Comm. Brechin. [NRS]

MITCHELL, DAVID, a greenman aboard the whaler Mary Ann of Dundee from Dundee to Greenland on 4 March 1813, abandoned the ship on return at Aberdeen to avoid the Press Gang on 16 August 1813. [NRS.E508.115.8]

MITCHELL, DAVID, son of John Mitchell in Montrose, graduated MA from Marischal College, Aberdeen, in 1821, later a teacher in Montrose. [MCA]

MITCHELL, GEORGE, master of the Swift of Dundee trading between St Petersburg, Russia, and Dundee in 1819. [NRS.E504.11.21]

MITCHELL, HANNAH, was found guilty of child murder in Rescobie and sentenced to 6 months imprisonment in 1850. [NRS.JC26.1850.569]

MITCHELL, JAMES, a clerk in the service of John Ogilvie a writer in Dundee, in 1792. [NRS.NRAS.124.4.2.59]

MITCHELL, JAMES, a shoemaker, was admitted as a burgess of Arbroath in 1799. [AA.18.941]

MITCHELL, JAMES, from Angus, graduated MA from King's College, Aberdeen, in March 1825. [KCA]

MITCHELL, JAMES, of the 3$^{rd}$ West Indian Regiment, his widow Margaret Sheret died 26 April 1844. [Montrose gravestone]

MITCHELL, JOHN, a shoemaker, was admitted as a burgess of Arbroath in 1797. [AA.18.941]

MITCHELL, JOHN, of Arngask, born 1803, died 7 June 1885, husband of Mary Easson, born 1800, died 14 July 1872. [Balgay gravestone, Dundee]

MITCHELL, JOHN, harpooner aboard the Dorothy of Dundee bound for the Davis Straits in 1825. [NRS.E508.130.8]

MITCHELL, PATRICK, a merchant in Dundee in 1798. [DCA.B19.3.27/15]

MITCHELL, ROBERT, fresh or green man aboard the Princess Charlotte of Dundee bound for the Davis Strait in 1824. [NRS.E508.129.8]

MITCHELL, Dr WILLIAM, born 1742, a physician in Dundee, died 1784, husband of Agnes Carnegy, born 1744, died 1825. [Howff gravestone, Dundee]

MITCHELSON, DAVID, born in Kirriemuir on 26 January 1732, admitted to the Scots Charitable Society of Boston in 1767 [SCS/NEHGS], 'late of New York', died at Fyfe Place, Leith Walk, Edinburgh, on 24 October 1802. [Canongait gravestone, Edinburgh]

MOCHAN, GEORGE, a weaver in Hilltown, Dundee, was accused of theft at Balgray, parish of Mains and Strathmartin, in 1837. [NRS.AD14.37.177]

MOIR, JOHN, a weaver, was admitted as a burgess of Arbroath in 1797. [AA.18.941]

MOIR, MARY, born 1758, daughter of William Moir of New Grange, died 4 July 1832. [St Vigeans gravestone]

MOLLISON, GEORGE, son of Alexander Mollison a minister in Montrose, graduated MA from Marischal College in 1794. [MCA]

MOLLISON, JAMES, in Viewbank, Forfar, graduated MD from King's College, Aberdeen, on 5 February 1814. [KCA]

MOLLISON, JOHN, former Provost of Brechin, testament, 1791, Comm. Brechin. [NRS]

MOLLESON, THOMAS, a burgess of Arbroath in 1800. [NRS.GD2.103]

MONCRIEFF, JAMES, master of the British King of Dundee a snow, in 1825. [DSR][DPCA.1201]

MONCUR, JAMES, a sailor aboard the whaler Mary Ann of Dundee from Dundee to Greenland on 4 March 1813, abandoned the ship on return at Aberdeen to avoid the Press Gang on 16 August 1813. [NRS.E508.115.8]

MONCUR, JOHN, line manager, of the Friendship of Dundee at the Davis Straits in 1824. [NRS.E508.130.8]

MONCUR, ROBERT, line manager aboard the Estridge of Dundee bound for the Davis Straits in 1824. [NRS.E508.129.8]

MONCUR, THOMAS, a glass and china merchant in Montrose in 1848. [NRS.CS280.10.44]

MONCUR, WILLIAM a fresh or green man aboard the Friendship of Dundee at the Davis Straits in 1824. [NRS.E508.130.8]

MONRO, THOMAS, in Overgait, Dundee, in 1798. [DCA.B19.3.27/11]

MORE, ALEXANDER, born 1762, died at sea in 1797. [Arbroath Abbey gravestone]

MORGAN, DAVID, born 1787, farmer at the Grange of Conan, died 8 October 1866, husband of Barbara Weir, born 1794, died 5 January 1865. [St Vigeans gravestone]

MORRIS, JAMES, a book seller in Brechin, died there on 2 July 1820. [SM.86.192]

MORRIS, THOMAS, master of the Betsy of Dundee died in St Petersburg, Russia, in1839. [MD.134]

MORRISON, ALEXANDER, a sawyer, was admitted as a burgess of Arbroath in 1797. [AA.18.941]

MORISON, ALEXANDER, a merchant in Dundee, an account book 1795-1797. [NRS.CS96.3840]

MORRISON, DAVID, a merchant and shipowner in Montrose, with his wife Elizabeth Mitchell from Aberdeen, settled in New Orleans, Louisiana, in 1790, died there in 1808. [ANY]

MORRISON, DUNCAN a Sergeant of the 3rd Regiment, was admitted as a burgess of Arbroath in 1797. [AA.18.941]

MORRISON, GEORGE a manufacturer, was admitted as a burgess of Arbroath in 1798. [AA.18.941]

MORISON, GEORGE, master of the Comely of Dundee, bound from Dundee to Charleston, South Carolina, in December 1818. [NRS.E504.11.21]

MORRISON, ROBERTSON, born 1773 in Dundee, died in Kingston, Jamaica, on 31 July 1794. [SM.56.655]

MORISON, WILLIAM, a merchant in Dundee, an account book, 1795-1797. [NRS.CS96.3840]

MORROW, WILLIAM, a sailor aboard the Dorothy of Dundee bound for the Davis Straits in 1825. [NRS.E508.130.8]

MORTON, MUNGO, a manufacturer in Dundee, in 1796. [DCA.B19.3.26/6]

MORTON, WILLIAM a weaver burgess of Arbroath in 1797. [AA.18.941]

MOUG, ALEXANDER, a manufacturer in Brechin, versus James Spaddie a smith in Ardovie, 1810. [NRS.CS36.1.54]

MOWAT, GEORGE, from Logie Pert, settled in New York city, probate 17 March 1796, N.Y.

MOWAT, JOHN, born 11 August 1740 in Montrose, son of Alexander Mowat and his wife Anne Walker, a cabinet maker and ironmonger in New York from 1777 to 1829, died there on 15 March 1829. [ANY]

MUAT, JAMES, the younger, a teacher in Edinburgh, by 1791 in Arbroath, a divorce. [NRS.C8.6.1068]

MUDIE, CHARLES, in Arbroath, versus John Airth the younger and Robert Rolland in 1820. [NRS.CS42.27.2]

MUDIE, GEORGE, born in Arbroath, was naturalised in South Carolina on 10 April 1820. [Circuit Court Journal, 9.56]

MUDIE, JAMES, a shipmaster in Dundee, testament, 1797, Comm. Brechin. [NRS]

MUDIE, JOHN, a stamp-master, was admitted as a burgess of Arbroath in 1798. [AA.18.941]

MUDIE, MARGARET, born 1779, died 1806, wife of William Bachelor a weaver on Hawkhill, Dundee. [Howff gravestone, Dundee]

MUGGINS, JAMES, in the Muirside of Kinnell in 1856. [AVR]

MUIR, ALEXANDER, a shipmaster, was admitted as a burgess of Arbroath in 1790. [AA.18.941]

MUIR, JAMES, born 1743, a shipmaster in Arbroath, died 1803, husband of Mary Dingwall, parents of James Muir born 1774, died

1806; testament, 1806, Comm. St Andrews. [NRS]; [Arbroath Abbey gravestone]

MUIR, JOHN, eldest son of Reverend John Muir in St Vigeans, died in Kingston, Jamaica, on 19 March 1848, an inventory, 1852. [NRS.SC70.1.74; E2879] [AJ.5287] [SG.18/1816]

MUNN, JAMES, a sailor aboard the whaler Mary Ann of Dundee from Dundee to Greenland on 4 March 1813, abandoned the ship on return at Aberdeen to avoid the Press Gang on 16 August 1813. [NRS.E508.115.8]

MUNRO, ALEXANDER, born 1811, a founder in Montrose, accused of housebreaking there in 1830. [NRS.AD14.30.68]

MUNRO, JOHN, a vintner in Dundee, testament, 1794, Comm. Brechin. [NRS]

MURDOCH, ALEXANDER, a burgess of Dundee in 1797, a skipper in Seagait, Dundee, master of the George of Dundee in 1797, [NRS.CE70.1.8/77]; master of the Rambler of Dundee in 1809, and of the Unity in 1818. [DD]

MURRAY, WILLIAM, a fresh or green man aboard the Estridge of Dundee bound for the Davis Straits in 1824. [NRS.E508.129.8]

MUSTARD, WILLIAM, a resident of the Seagait, Dundee, a ship's mate in Dundee in 1796, aboard the sloop Isabella of Dundee from Riga, Latvia, to Dundee. [NRS.CE70.1.8/4]; master of the Dispatch of Dundee in 1809, and of the Eliza of Dundee trading between Riga and Dundee in 1818. [DD][NRS.E504.11.21]

MYERS, ALEXANDER, from Forfar, graduated MA from King's College, Aberdeen, in March 1831. [KCA]

MYERS, CHARLES, born on British Heligoland in 1818, cook aboard the Narwhal 1837, husband of Agnes. [HS.18.1.20]

MYLES, ALEXANDER, born 1761, a skipper on the West Shore, Dundee, in 1782, and in Tindall's Wynd, Dundee, in 1818, [DD]; master of the Helen of Dundee in 1794, [NRS.CE70.1.8/7]; of the Augusta in 1818, [DD]; died in 1828, husband of Catherine Meldrum. [Howff gravestone, Dundee]

NAIRN, CHARLES, a weaver, was admitted as a burgess of Arbroath in 1797. [AA.18.941]

NAIRN, DAVID, in Rescobie, was a victim of theft when aboard the steamer Thane of Fife in 1850. [NRS.AD14.50.492; JC26.1850.569]

NAIRN, JAMES, a weaver burgess of Arbroath in 1798. [AA.18.941]

NAIRN, JOHN, born 1735, a shipmaster in Dundee, died 1812, husband of Anne Watson, born 1810, died 1760. [Howff gravestone, Dundee]

NAIRN, THOMAS, a shipmaster in Dundee, testament, 1799, Comm. Brechin. [NRS]

NAISMITH, JOHN, born 22 March 1726 in Dundee, son of Robert Naismith and his wife Jean Young, a Jacobite prisoner transported to Maryland in 1747, later a mail carrier in Euston, Maryland, died on 20 August 1796. [P.3.224][TNA.T1.328][Maryland Herald, 27.8.1793]

NAPIER, ADAM, from Montrose, a student in Marischal College in 1790s. [MCA]

NAPIER, JOSEPH, a merchant, was admitted as a burgess of Arbroath in 1792. [AA.18.941]

NAPIER, MARGARET, eldest daughter of Dr Robert Napier of Grenada and of Bervie, Kincardineshire, died in Montrose on 24 April 1863. [S.2450]

NEAVE, THOMAS, born 1734, died 1813. [Howff gravestone, Dundee]

NEISH, CHARLES, a merchant in Arbroath, trading with Riga, Latvia, in 1811. [NRS.CS36.1.12]

NEISH, DAVID, born 1804, son of John Neish and his wife Susan Robertson, died in Jamaica on 17 February 1817. [Trottick gravestone]

NEISH, JOHN, son of John Neish and his wife Susan Robertson, died in Jamaica on 27 September 1831. [Trottick gravestone]

NEISH, WILLIAM, a farmer in Arbroath, testament, 1791, Comm. St Andrews. [NRS]

NEISH and SMART, merchants in Dundee, trading with Latvia and Russia between 1826 and 1827. [NRS.CS96.3731]

NESS, ALEXANDER, steersman aboard the Estridge of Dundee bound for the Davis Straits in 1824. [NRS.E508.129.8]

NESS, JAMES, sailor aboard the Estridge of Dundee bound for the Davis Straits in 1824. [NRS.E508.129.8]

NICHOLL, DAVID, a merchant burgess of Dundee in 1797, at the East Port of Dundee, husband of Margaret Scott born 1743, died 1821. [NRS.NRAS.1684/9] [Howff gravestone, Dundee]

NICHOL, JAMES and DAVIDSON, booksellers and stationers in Montrose, 1845. [NRS.CS280.7.48]

NICHOLSON, RICHARD, a journeyman carpenter in Dundee, was accused of assault in 1819. [NRS.AD14.19.167]

NICOLL, DAVID, at Aucheen, Lochlee, testament, 1799, Comm. Brechin. [NRS]

NICOLL, DAVID, born 1737, a manufacturer in Dundee, died 1807, husband of Janet Begbie. [Howff gravestone, Dundee]

NICOLL, DAVID, born 3 May 1847, son of James and Jane Nicoll, a shipmaster who died in Port Townsend, Washington, on 14 January 1897. [Monifieth gravestone]

NICOLL, DONALD, born 1714, in Aucheen, Lochlee, died 9 October 1799, testament, 1799, Comm. Brechin. [NRS][Lochlee gravestone]

NICOLL, GEORGE, late in Jamaica, then in Dundee in 1790. [DCA.B19.3.27/9]EC.14292]

NICOLL, JAMES, in Dundee, exported a cargo of linen aboard the Perceval, Captain Scott, bound for New York in April 1820. [NRS.E04.11.21]

NICOL, JOHN, a writer, was admitted as a burgess of Arbroath in 1797. [AA.18.941]

NICOLL, JOHN, an officer of the Dean of Guild in Dundee in 1798. [DCA. B19.3.27/6]

NICOLL, JOHN, from Dundee, died in Kingston, Jamaica, on 25 April 1803. [E

NICOLL, JOHN, son of James Nicoll a mason in Dundee, settled in Kingston, Jamaica, was admitted as a burgess of Dundee on 15 November 1823. [DBR]

NICOL, JOHN, sailor aboard the Princess Charlotte of Dundee bound for the Davis Strait in 1824. [NRS.E508.129.8]

NICOLL, JOSEPH, from Montrose, married Isabella Hogg from Wemyss, Fife, in Montreal on 24 April 1860. [Fife Free Press]

NICOL, ROBERT, a smith, was admitted as a burgess of Arbroath in 1797. [AA.18.941]

NICOLL, ROBERT, a weaver in Carnoustie, a tack, 1840. [NRS.GD45.16]

NICOLL, SAMUEL, a cattle dealer in Kirriemuir, sederunt book, 1829-1838. [NRS.CS96.4284]

NICOLL, WILLIAM, a skipper in Butcher Row, Dundee, in 1806, in 88 Murraygait, Dundee, in 1818, master of the Hope of Dundee in 1796, of the Eliza of Dundee in 1809, and the Antelope in 1818. [DD]; master of the Antelope of Dundee trading between Riga and Dundee in 1819. [NRS.E504.11.21]

NICOLL, WILLIAM, a wright in Arbirlot, a tack, 1840. [NRS.GD45.16.1732]

NICOLSON, JOHN, a bleacher in Trottick, parish of Mains and Strathmartine, was accused of assaulting officers of the law in 1837. [NRS.AD14.37.122]

NICHOLSON, NEIL, a bleacher of Turnbull and Company at Claverhouse bleachfield, Trottick, parish of Mains and Strathmartine, was accused of assaulting officers of the law in 1837. [NRS.AD14.37.122]

NISBET, ....., son of Charles Nisbet and his wife Anne Tweedie, emigrated to America in 1784, a judge in Baltimore, Maryland, died 22 November 1857. [NARA.M432/277-299] [Montrose, Md., gravestone]

NISBET, Reverend Dr CHARLES, former minister in Montrose, Principal of Dickenson College in Pennsylvania, died in America in 1804. [AM.66.479]

NIVEN, JOHN, in Peebles by Arbroath, was admitted as a burgess of Arbroath in 1790. [AA.18.941]

NORRIE, ADAM, born 13 February 1796 in Montrose, settled in New York by 1827, died there on 6 June 1882. [ANY]

NORRIE, DAVID, fresh or green man aboard the Princess Charlotte of Dundee bound for the Davis Strait in 1824. [NRS.E508.129.8]

NORRIE, GEORGE, a skipper in Crichton Street, Dundee, 1809, master of the Jean of Dundee in 1799, [NRS.CE70.1.8]; testament, 1835, [NRS.SC45.31.3.7]

NUCATOR, PETER, a skipper in Fish Street, Dundee, in 1809, and in Perth Road, Dundee, by 1808, [DD]; master of the Patience in 1794, [NRS.CE70.1.8/83], of the Betsey of Dundee from 1807 to 1809, [DPCA.309][DW.263], and the Susanna in 1818, [DD].

OCHTERLONY, JOHN, born 1743, Provost of Arbroath, died in 1804, husband of Isabella ...., born 1739, died 1818. [Arbroath Abbey gravestone]

OCHTERLONY, JOHN, of Guynd, versus Thomas Mason, the minister of Dunnichen, in 1808. [NRS.CS271.58762]

OGG, ALEXANDER, a draper in Brechin, sederunt books, 1826-1827, [NRS.CS96.400-401]

OGILVY, ADAM, youngest son of Sir John Ogilvy, died in Antigua on 29 July 1799. [SM.61.724]

OGILVIE, ANDREW, born 1790, a farm manager in Kirriemuir, was jointly accused of the culpable homicide of James Ogilvy at Wheen, Cortachy, in 1830. [NRS.AD14.30.9]

OGILVIE, CHARLES, born 1813, son of David Ogilvy of Parkconon, Montrose, died at Port Stanley, London, Upper Canada, on 25 January 1838. [NBC.10.3.1838] [Montrose gravestone]

OGILVIE, DAVID, born 1795 in Brechin, a stonecutter, died in St John, New Brunswick, on 9 January 1828. [NBC.12.1.1828]

OGILVIE, DAVID, master of the Olive of Dundee trading between Danzig, Prussia, and Dundee in 1819. [NRS.E504.11.21]

OGILVIE, DAVID, steersman on board the Princess Charlotte of Dundee bound for the Davis Strait in 1824. [NRS.E508.129.8]

OGILVIE, DAVID, [2], apprentice aboard the Princess Charlotte of Dundee bound for the Davis Strait in 1824. [NRS.E508.129.8]

OGILVIE, DAVID, from Kirriemuir, graduated MA from King's College, Aberdeen, in March 1845. [KCA]

OGILVIE, GEORGE, a merchant in Dundee, in 1799. [DCA.B19.3.27/162]

OGILVIE, GEORGE, late of Jamaica, later in Dundee by 1800. [DCA.H187]

OGILVY, GEORGE RAMSAY, of Westhall, born 1822, died 22 November 1866, husband of Mary Christina Bachar who died on 30 October 1879. [Murroes gravestone]

OGILVIE, Mrs HANNAH, a resident of Charleston, South Carlina, before 1776, a Loyalist, wife of Henry Ogilvie a shipmaster in the service of the Honourable East India Company deceased, via Jamaica with her children to Dundee by 1784. [TNA.AO13.133.223]

OGILVY, HENRY, a shipmaster in Charleston, South Carolina, died 1779, son of Henry Ogilvy of Templehall, and wife of Hannah Meadows, testament, 1784, Comm. Edinburgh. [NRS]

OGILVY, HENRY, from Dundee, died in Pensacola, Florida, probate 1785, PCC. [TNA]

OGILVY, ISABELL, from Kinnettles, later in Glamis, versus Alexander Lunan from Invereighty, a Process of Declarator of Marriage, 1820. [NRS.CC8.6.1753]

OGILVIE, JAMES, sailor aboard the Princess Charlotte of Dundee bound for the Davis Strait in 1824. [NRS.E508.129.8]

OGILVIE, JAMES, born 1771, a skipper in Castle Street, Dundee, master of the Grafton of Dundee in 1795, and of the Olive in 1818, died in 1834, testament, 1835, [NRS.NRS.SC45.31.2.356]

OGILVIE, JAMES, second son of James Ogilvie a writer in Dundee, was educated at Glasgow University, a commission agent in New York, died in Dundee in 1836, testament, 1837. [NRS.SC70.1.56] [ANY]

OGILVIE, JOHN, a writer in Dundee, in 1799. [DCA.B19.3.27/202]

OGILVY, JOHN, a planter in St Mary's, Middlesex County, Jamaica, appointed William Ogilvy in Kirriemuir as his attorney in 1802. [NRS.RD3.300.1112]

OGILVIE, JOHN, son of William Ogilvie of Glenogilvie, a student at Marischal College in 1808. [MCA]

OGILVIE, JOHN KINLOCH, born 1813, a hand loom weaver in Carnoustie, died 24 August 1895, husband of Ann Cant, born 1814, died 31 August 1895. [Barry gravestone]

OGILVIE, JOHN, born 1814, a shipmaster, died at Buddon Ness Lights on 19 February 1874, husband of Amelia Guthrie Begg, born 1817, died 6 April 1899. [Barry gravestone]

OGILVIE, KATHERINE, daughter of Henry Ogilvie a vintner in Dundee, testament, 1793, Comm. Brechin. [NRS]

OGILVIE, MATTHEW, born 1809, a merchant who emigrated from Dundee on the Herald bound for Charleston, South Carolina, landed there in October 1826. [NARA]

OGILVIE, THOMAS, a tacksman in Northmuir, Kirriemuir, was jointly accused of the culpable homicide of James Ogilvy at Wheen, Cortachy, in 1830. [NRS.AD14.30.9]

OGILVIE, WALTER, son of Reverend Thomas Ogilvie in Kirriemuir, graduated MA from Marischal College in 1812, later a surgeon in the service of the East India Company. [MCA]

OGILVIE, WILLIAM, emigrated to South Carolina in 1764, Secretary to the Superintendent of Indian Affairs for the Southern District until 1775, a Loyalist, later a merchant in London, settled in Newtonmill, Forfar, by 1790. [TNA.AO12.47.141, etc]

OLIPHANT, MATTHEW, sailor aboard the Estridge of Dundee bound for the Davis Straits in 1824. [NRS.E508.129.8]

ORCHARD, ALEXANDER, steersman aboard the Dorothy of Dundee bound for the Davis Straits in 1825. [NRS.E508.130.8]

ORCHARD, JAMES, steersman aboard the Dorothy of Dundee bound for the Davis Straits in 1825. [NRS.E508.130.8]

ORMOND, ALEXANDER, master of the Active of Dundee in 1809. [DD]

OSLER, WILLIAM, from Dunnichen, graduated MA from King's College, Aberdeen, in April 1860, later a farmer in Dunnichen. [KCA]

OSWALD, JOHN, steersman aboard the Estridge of Dundee bound for the Davis Straits in 1824. [NRS.E508.129.8]

OUCHTERLONY, JOHN, of the Guynd, father of John Ouchterlony a merchant in Riga, Latvia, in 1793. [NRS.S/H]

OUCHTERLONY, MARJORIE, daughter of John Ouchterlony a merchant in Montrose, testament, 1797, Comm. Brechin. [NRS]

OUCHTERLONY, MARY, from the Guynd in Angus, settled Riga, Latvia, before 1844. [NRS.S/H]

OXLEY, JONAS, born in Montrose, an officer of the 3$^{rd}$ West Indian Regiment, later in the service of the Hudson Bay Company from 1819 until 1822. [HBRS]

PARIS, ANDREW, a shipmaster in Carnoustie, a tack, 1840. [NRS.GD45.16]

PARIS, GEORGE, a seaman in Carnoustie, a tack, 1840. [NRS.GD45.16]

PARIS, JOHN, son of Robert Paris in Westhaven, a victim of theft in 1837. [NRS.AD14.37.117]

PARKIE, ALEXANDER, steersman aboard the Princess Charlotte of Dundee bound for the Davis Strait in 1824. [NRS.E508.129.8]

PATON, DAVID, son of John Paton a merchant in Montrose, a student at Marischal College, Aberdeen, in 1824, later a Free Church minister in Fettercairn. [MCA]

PATON, JOHN, a burgess of Dundee in 1794, [DBR]; a skipper in St Clement's Lane, Dundee, in 1809, [DD]; master of the Sprightly of Dundee in 1809. [DD]

PATON, NEIL, a labourer in Monikie, was accused of murder in 1847. [NRS.AD14.47.120]

PATON, ROBERT, born 1773, a shoemaker in Carnoustie, died 13 November 1829, husband of Helen Milln, born 1775, died 28 March 1839. [Barry gravestone]

PATON, WILLIAM, a weaver, was admitted as a burgess of Arbroath in 1797. [AA.18.941]

PATON, WILLIAM, a coal merchant in Panbride in May 1831. [NRS.CS46.1831.5.56]

PATTERSON, ALEXANDER, born 1761, died in Montrose on 7 July 1820. [SM.86.192]

PATERSON, ALEXANDER, son of Reverend Alexander Paterson in Dundee, graduated MA from Marischal College, Aberdeen, in 1821. [MCA]

PATTERSON, CHARLES, a flax-dresser, was admitted as a burgess of Arbroath in 1798. [AA.18.941]

PATERSON, DAVID, from Montrose, graduated MD from King's College, Aberdeen, on 18 April 1801. [KCA]

PATTERSON, GEORGE, a shipmaster, was admitted as a burgess of Arbroath in 1795. [AA.18.941]

PATTERSON, JAMES, a baker and corn merchant of Arbroath from 1789 to 1798. [NRS.CS96.3223]

PATERSON, JAMES, a merchant in Overgait, Dundee, in 1798. [DCA.B19.3.27/11]

PATTERSON, JAMES, a fresh or green man aboard the Estridge of Dundee bound for the Davis Straits in 1824. [NRS.E508.129.8]

PATTERSON, WILLIAM, master of the Jeffry of Dundee in 1809. [DD]

PATTERSON, ....., a wright, was admitted as a burgess of Arbroath in 1797. [AA.18.941]

PATTIE, ROBERT, harpooner aboard the Dorothy of Dundee bound for the Davis Straits in 1825. [NRS.E508.130.8]

PATTON, HENRY, a hatter in Dundee in 1799. [DCA.B19.3.27/268]

PATTULLO, GEORGE, born 1803, a farmer in East Downie, was buried in Monikie on 16 May 1848. [Monikie Burial Register]

PATTULLO, ROBERT, a shipmaster in Murraygait, Dundee, 1782. [DD]; master of the Active in 1775. [NRS.E504.11.9]

PEACOCK, DAVID, a weaver, was admitted as a burgess of Arbroath in 1797. [AA.18.941]

PEARSON, JAMES, sailor aboard the Dorothy of Dundee bound for the Davis Straits in 1825. [NRS.E508.130.8]

PEDDIE, ANDREW, born 1744, a merchant in Dundee, died 1810, husband of Elizabeth How, born 1750. Died 1819. [Howff gravestone, Dundee]

PEDDIE, ROBERT, head harpooner aboard the Friendship in 1837, husband of Margaret Stiven. [HS.18.1.20]

PENN, ANDREW, a pavier in Dundee, testament 1794, Comm. Brechin. [NRS]

PENNY, JOHN, a mechanic in Session Street, Dundee, was accused of mobbing and rioting in the New Hall, Bell Street, Dundee, in 1842. [NRS.AD14.42.354; JC26.1843.443]

PENNYCOOK, GILBERT, a merchant in Brechin, 1809. [NRS.CS230.SEQN.P1.8]

PERRY, FREDERICK, from Montrose, graduated MA from King's College, Aberdeen, in March 1845. [KCA]

PETER, ALEXANDER, a tailor, was admitted as a burgess of Arbroath in 1797. [AA.18.941]

PETER, DAVID, a blacksmith in Scouringburn, Dundee, accused of armed robbery in 1840. [NRS.AD14.40.295]

PETER, GEORGE, master of the Fairy of Dundee from Cromarty and Thurso with passengers to Pictou, Nova Scotia, and Quebec in 1835 and 1841. [JJ.5.2.1841][MG]

PETER, JOHN, a tailor, was admitted as a burgess of Arbroath in 1797. [AA.18.941]

PETER, JOHN, born 1738, a builder in Dundee in 1799, died 1813, husband of Mary Hog, born 1734, died 1794. [Howff gravestone, Dundee] [NRS.SCCC20.33.1] [DCA.B19.3.27/266]

PETER, WALTER, a merchant in Dykehead, Cortachy, testament, 1791, Comm. Brechin. [NRS]

PETER, WILLIAM, a tailor, was admitted as a burgess of Arbroath in 1797. [AA.18.941]

PETTICREW, JOHN, fresh or green man aboard the Princess Charlotte of Dundee bound for the Davis Strait in 1824. [NRS.E508.129.8]

PETRIE, ALEXANDER, a weaver, was admitted as a burgess of Arbroath in 1797. [AA.18.941]

PETRIE, ALEXANDER, was admitted as a burgess of Arbroath in 1797. [AA.18.941]

PETRIE, DAVID, a brass founder, a tack of lands in Monifieth in 1842. [NRS.GD45.16.2078]

PETRIE, JAMES, a wright, was admitted as a burgess of Arbroath in 1798. [AA.18.941]

PETRIE, JAMES STURROCK, born 2 March 1809 in Arbroath, son of John H. Petrie, a merchant in New York until his death in 1860. [ANY]

PETRIE, JAMES, son of Henry Petrie, [1752-1833], and his wife Helen Douglas, [17751859], died in Melbourne, Australia, in 1859. [St Andrew's gravestone, Dundee]

PETRIE, JOHN, a manufacturer, was admitted as a burgess of Arbroath in 1799 [AA.18.941]

PETRIE, JOHN, son of Henry Petrie and his wife Helen Douglas, died in Meadville, USA, in 1833. [St Andrew's gravestone, Dundee]

PETRIE, MARGARET, in Cononsyth, Carmyllie, victim of a bigamous marriage, 1836. [NRS.AD14.36.74]

PHILIPS, ADAM, jr., son of Adam Philips tacksman of the tollbar of Inchbrayoch, found guilty of murder, sentenced to 12 months in Forfar Tolbooth in 1818. [NRS.JC26.1818.109]

PHILIPS, ALEXANDER, a boat-builder in Dundee, husband of Catherine Crombie, born 1762, died 1792. [Howff gravestone, Dundee]

PHILIPS, JAMES, master of the Thistle of Montrose trading with Inverness in 1811. [NRS.E504.17.8]

PHILLIPS, Major WILLIAM, born 1744, died 1813, husband of Catherine Nicoll, born 1744, died 1811. [Howff gravestone, Dundee]

PHILP, DAVID, born 1805, a carpenter who emigrated from Dundee on the Herald bound for Charleston, South Carolina, landed there in November 1827. [NARA]

PHIN, A. C., born 1811 in Dundee, a druggist in Charleston, South Carolina, naturalised there on 13 January 1847. [NARA.M1183.1]

PILMORE, JAMES, son of William Pilmore in Montrose, graduated MA from Marischal College, Aberdeen, in 1810. [MCA]

RINTOUL, ALEXANDER, master of the Anna of Dundee trading between Stockholm, Sweden, and Dundee in 1818. [NRS.E504.11.21]

PIRIE, ALEXANDER, in Overgait, Dundee, was accused of robbing, rioting and assaulting army officers at Dudhope Barracks, Dundee, in 1832. [NRS.AD14.32.29]

PIRIE, GILBERT, a weaver in Hilltown, Dundee, husband of May Mudie, born 1752, died 1812. [Howff gravestone, Dundee]

PIRIE, JAMES, from Angus, graduated MA from King's College, Aberdeen, on26 March 1790. [KCA]

PIRIE, JAMES, a fireman of the Dundee and Newtyle Railway Company, Hatton Hill, Newtyle, was accused of culpable homicide in 1836. [NRS.AD14.36.89]

PIRIE, JOHN, a minister in Lochlee parish, a letter, 1803. [NRS.GD45.13.157]

PIRIE, JOHN, a fresh or green man aboard the Dorothy of Dundee bound for the Davis Straits in 1825. [NRS.E508.130.8]

PITCAIRN, ANDREW, a writer in Dundee in 1798. [DCA.B19.3.27/11]

PITCAIRN, JOHN, a writer in Dundee in 1766, died in 1800. [NRS.CS16.1.125/247] [Howff gravestone, Dundee]

PITCAITHLY, MARGARET, born 1827, wife of George Bruce, died in Christchurch, New Zealand, on 26 May 1876. [Kettins gravestone]

PITHIE, ROBERT, a hay dresser, was admitted as a burgess of Arbroath in 1797. [AA.18.941]

PLAYFAIR, THOMAS, born 1742, a brewer in Seagait, Dundee, died 1809. [Howff gravestone, Dundee]

POTTER, JOHN, born 1819, a manufacturer in Lochee, died 12 September 1885, husband of Margaret Camley, born 1800, died 20 November 1890. [Balgay gravestone, Dundee]

PRAIN, WILLIAM, sailor aboard the Estridge of Dundee bound for the Davis Straits in 1824. [NRS.E508.129.8]

PRIOR, ALEXANDER, a carter, was admitted as a burgess of Arbroath in 1791. [AA.18.941]

PROCTOR, GEORGE, son of Patrick Proctor in Glamis, Secretary to the Medical Board, and surgeon to the Presidency of Calcutta, India, died there in July 1825. [SM.97.254]

PROCTOR, JAMES, born 1785, a manufacturer in Forfar, died in Barry on 30 July 1850, husband of Isabella Innes, born 1773, died in Barry on 12 December 1857. [Barry gravestone]

PROCTOR, JAMES, from Forfar, graduated MA from King's College, Aberdeen, in March 1838. [KCA]

PROCTOR, JOHN, a sawyer, was admitted as a burgess of Arbroath in 1797. [AA.18.941]

PROFIT, CHARLES, from Dundee, settled in New Orleans, Louisiana, by 1805. [NRS.CS17.1.24E/161]

PRYDE, ALEXANDER, sailor aboard the Princess Charlotte of Dundee bound for the Davis Strait in 1824. [NRS.E508.129.8]

PYOTT, or MAITLAND, JAMES, son of James Pyott a merchant in Montrose, a merchant in New York, deeds in 1797, 1798. [NRS.RD4.263.1084; CS17.1.17/20]

RAE, WILLIAM, master of the George of Dundee trading between Leith and Savanna, Georgia, in 1840. [S.24/2163]

RAITT, DAVID, a skipper in 29 Murraygait, Dundee, [DD], master of the Jessie of Dundee in 1799, [NRS.CE70.1.8]; master of the Nymph of Dundee in 1809, of the Salamanca in 1818, testament, 1823, [NRS.CC3.15.4481]

RAITT, WILLIAM, a surgeon in Dundee, testament, 1795, Comm. Brechin. [NRS]

RAMSAY, ALEXANDER, a surgeon in Broughty Ferry, a tack of land in Barnhill in 1848. [NRS.GD45.16.2088]

RAMSAY, DAVID, an apprentice roper in Dundee, was accused of mobbing and rioting in 1816. [NRS.AD14.16.58]

RAMSAY, GEORGE, in Arbroath, died 19 September 1864, grandfather of James Kyd Smart in Chicago, Illinois, his heir in 1896. [NRS.S/H]

RAMSAY, JAMES, born in Arbroath, settled in Patterson, New Jersey, died on the Columbia when bound from New York to Glasgow. [S.7504]

RAMSAY, JAMES, in Carnoustie, a tack, 1840. [NRS.GD45.16]

RAMSAY, JOHN, of Kinnalty, father of John Ramsay a Lieutenant of the Scotch Brigade in Dutch Service, a sasine, 1782. [NRS.R.S.Forfar.181]

RAMSAY, JOHN, a manufacturer, was admitted as a burgess of Arbroath in 1797. [AA.18.941]

RAMSAY, ROBERT, son of Reverend William Ramsay in Cortachy, graduated MA from Marischal College, Aberdeen, in 1804, later an assistant surgeon of the Royal Artillery. [MCA]

RAMSAY, WILLIAM, a weaver, was admitted as a burgess of Arbroath in 1797. [AA.18.941]

RAMSAY, WILLIAM, son of Reverend William Ramsay in Cortachy, a student at Marischal College in 1809, later a minister in Alyth. [MCA]

RAMSAY, WILLIAM, a carpenter in Dundee, was accused of assault in 1819. [NRS.AD14.19.167]

RAMSAY, WILLIAM, a shoemaker, a tack, 1840. [NRS.GD45.16]

RANKINE, JAMES, a planter and merchant in Jamaica from 1788 to 1814, later a merchant in Dundee from 1819 to 1820. [NRS.CS230.Sed.book 4/2]

RATTRAY, CHARLES, born 1835, son of William Rattray and his wife Maggie Smith Moir, died at Bluff Harbour, New Zealand, on 26 June 1885. [Arbroath Abbey gravestone]

RATTRAY, DAVID, born 1760, a manufacturer in Dundee, died 1811, husband of Mary Scott. [Howff gravestone, Dundee]

RATTRAY, JOHN, master of the Hercules of Dundee in 1809. [DD]

RATTRAY, WILLIAM, son of William Rattray a weaver in Lochee, a student at Marischal College, Aberdeen, in 1846, later a schoolmaster in Aberdeen and in Derbyshire. [MCA]

REACH, ALEXANDER, line manager aboard the Dorothy of Dundee bound for the Davis Straits in 1825. [NRS.E508.130.8]

REACH, FRANCIS, a fresh or green man aboard the Dorothy of Dundee bound for the Davis Straits in 1825. [NRS.E508.130.8]

REID, ALEXANDER, master of the Hector of Dundee from Dundee to New York in 1837. [DPCA.1798]

REID, CHARLES, born 4 April 1800 in Forfar, son of George Reid, a grocer, and his wife Elizabeth Taylor, emigrated in 1801, settled in Portsmouth and Norfolk, Virginia, before 1827, died in Norfolk, Va., on 17 January 1899. [ANY.2.261][NARA M932-982][LNA.149]

REID, DAVID, born in Forfar, was naturalised in Craven County, North Carolina, on 8 August 1825. [Craven County Court Records, N.C.]

REID, GEORGE, a carter in Dundee, testament, 1791, Comm. Brechin. [NRS]

REID, GEORGE, son of William Reid and his wife Elizabeth Taylor in Forfar, emigrated to America in 1801, settled in Norfolk, Virginia, was naturalised on 28 September 1808 there, died in 1849. [CF.7.392]

REID, JAMES, master of the Hope of Dundee trading between Ballachulish and Inverness in 1814. [NRS.E504.17.8]

REID, JOHN, a sailor aboard the Friendship of Dundee at the Davis Straits in 1824. [NRS.E508.130.8]

REID, ROBERT, a candlemaker, was admitted as a burgess of Arbroath in 1795. [AA.18.941]

REID, WILLIAM, son of John Reid a schoolmaster in Kirriemuir, a sudent at Marischal College, Aberdeen, around 1816. [MCA]

REID, WILLIAM, from Forfar, graduated MA from King's College, Aberdeen, in March 1845. [KCA]

REIKIE, NIEL, sailor aboard the Princess Charlotte of Dundee bound for the Davis Strait in 1824. [NRS.E508.129.8]

RENNY, ALEXANDER, eldest son of Robert Renny a merchant in Jamaica, was granted Borrowfield, Montrose, on 21 December 1795. [NRA.RGS.128.148]

RENNY, ALLAN KENNY, born 1823, an accountant of the Union Bank of Australia, died in Melbourne on 11 March 1846. [Arbroath Abbey gravestone]

RENNIE, CHARLES, son of Henry Rennie in Montrose, graduated MA from Marischal College, Aberdeen, in 1808, later a srgeon. [MCA]

RENNY, GEORGE, born 10 April 1789, a Lieutenant in the Royal Navy, died 12 August 1809 of Flushing, [Vlissingen in the Netherlands] 'in the service of his country'. [Montrose gravestone]

RENNY, JAMES, a shipmaster in Montrose, testament, 1796, Comm. Brechin. [NRS]

RENNY, JAMES, late in Jamaica, probate, 1800, PCC. [TNA]

RENNY, ROBERT, late of Jamaica, then in Montrose, 1787. [GA.TD219/6]

RENNY, ROBERT, born 28 February 1785, Lieutenant Colonel of the 21st Regiment, died on 8 January 1815 at the Battle of New Orleans. [Montrose gravestone]

RENNY, SAMUEL, a cloth merchant in Arbroath, sederunt book, 1816-1817. [NRS.CS96.405]

RICHARDSON, JAMES, born 1800, a mason, died 12 December 1866, husband of Jane Sturrock, born 1799, died 21 May 1841. [St Vigeans gravestone]

RIDDOCH, ALEXANDER, born 1744, Provost of Dundee, and Deputy Lieutenant of Angus, died 1822. [Howff gravestone, Dundee]

RIDDOCH, MARY, born 1791, with Margaret Riddoch born 1814, and Jessie Riddoch born 1816, emigrated from Dundee on the Herald bound for Charleston, South Carolina, landed there in October 1826. [NARA]

RINTOUL, AGNES, third daughter of John Rintoul of Montrose Academy, married Reverend Milo Templeton from Troy, Miami County, Ohio, in Alleghany City, Pennsylvania, on 3 August 1846. [AJ.5747]

RINTOUL, ALEXANDER, a skipper in Crichton Street, Dundee, in 1809, [DD], master of the Earl of Cassils in 1809, and of the Anna of Dundee in 1818, [DD]trading between Rotterdam, Zealand, and Dundee in 1819, [NRS.E504.11.21]; of the Forfarshire of Dundee in 1824, and of the Glasgow of Dundee in 1825. [DSR]

RINTOUL, JOHN, son of John Rintoul headmaster in Montrose, graduated MA from Marischal College, Aberdeen, in 1831. [MCA]

RITCHIE, ALEXANDER, a merchant burgess of Arbroath, 1781, 1795. [AA.18.941][NRS.CS96.2037]

RITCHIE, ALEXANDER, in Brechin, 1817. [NRS.GD45.23.225]

RITCHIE, DAVID, master of the Fairy of Dundee from Dundee with passengers to Quebec in 1833, 1834, 1835. [DPCA][QM]

RITCHIE, JEAN, wife of Donald McCraw a malt maker in Brechin Road, Arbroath, found guilty of theft was sentenced to transportation to the colonies for ten years in 1845. [NRS.JC26.1845.418]

RITCHIE, JOHN, senior, a merchant in Arbroath, sederunt books, 1829-1831. [NRS.CS96.403]

RITCHIE, PATRICK, born 27 January 1738, a manufacturer in Arbroath who was admitted as a freeman and guilds-brother of Arbroath in 1774, a weaver burgess of Arbroath in 1797, died 29 March 1805. [AA.18.941][AA.X.98][Arbroath Abbey gravestone]

RITCHIE, SUSAN MURRAY, born 24 May 1828, daughter of George Ritchie and his wife Hope Keir, wife of James Dickson, died in Waikato, Warrnambool, Victoria, Australia, on 26 June 1870. [Arbroath Abbey gravestone]

ROB, DAVID, son of David Rob and his wife Margaret Spink, a shipmaster in Arbroath, who died in 1805, testament, 1806, Comm. St Andrews. [NRS][Arbroath Abbey gravestone]

ROBB, ELIZABETH, in Dundee, was accused of mobbing and rioting in 1816. [NRS.AD14.16.58]

ROBB, JAMES, from Angus, graduated MA from King's College, Aberdeen, on 25 March 1814. [KCA]

ROBB....., master of the Advice in 1853. [DD]

ROBBIE, JAMES, son of Charles Robbie and his wife Elizabeth McKenzie, settled in Australia before 1865. [Kirriemuir gravestone]

ROBBIE, WILLIAM, son of Charles Robbie and his wife Elizabeth McKenzie, settled in Australia before 1865. [Kirriemuir gravestone]

ROBERTS, Reverend JAMES, born 25 December 1839 in Montrose, emigrated with his parents to America in August 1850, settled on the Brandywine near Wilmington, Delaware, a Presbyterian minister in New Jersey and in Pennsylvania, died 27 September 1906, buried in Oakland cemetery, West Chester, Pennsylvania. [AP.303]

ROBERT, PETER, a baker, was admitted as a burgess of Arbroath in 1795. [AA.18.941]

ROBERTSON, ADAM, born 1784, a painter who died in Charleston, South Carolina, on 9 December 1838. [Arbroath Abbey gravestone]

ROBERTSON, DAVID, a boat-builder in Dundee in 1796. [DCA.B19.24.1.50]

ROBERTSON, DAVID, a weaver, was admitted as a burgess of Arbroath in 1797. [AA.18.941]

ROBERTSON, DAVID, born 1821, son of George Robertson, [1793-1865], and his wife Maria Esther Ireland, [1797-1844], died in Sacramento City, California, on 29 June 1850. [Eastern Necropolis gravestone, Dundee]

ROBERTSON, FRANCIS, a merchant in Montrose, testament, 1800, Comm. Brechin. [NRS]

ROBERTSON, JAMES, a writer in Edinburgh, later in Montrose, testament, 1793. Comm. Brechin. [NRS]

ROBERTSON, JAMES, born 1726, a thread-maker in Dundee, died in 1798. [Howff gravestone, Dundee]

ROBERTSON, JAMES, sailor aboard the Estridge of Dundee, bound for the Davis Straits in 1824. [NRS.E508.129.8]

ROBERTSON, JAMES, jr., a potato and oatmeal dealer in Benvie, victim of an armed robbery in 1840. [NRS.AD14.4Q.295]

ROBERTSON, JAMES, born 25 December 1839 in Montrose, emigrated with his parents to America in August 1850, settled on the Brandywine near Wilmington, Delaware, a Presbyterian minister in New Jersey and in Pennsylvania, died 27 December 1906, buried in Oakland Cemetery, West Chester, Pa. [AP]

ROBERTSON, JOHN, a hay-dresser, was admitted as a burgess of Arbroath in 1797. [AA.18.941]

ROBERTSON, JOHN, a skipper in Blackscroft, Dundee, master of the True Blue of Dundee in 1809, of the Union of Dundee in 1809, [DD], of the Farmer of Dundee from 1818 to 1825. [DSR]

ROBERTSON, ROBERT, born 1721, a musician, died 1808, husband of [1] Chirsten Drummond, born 1736, died 1776, [2] Agnes Coupar, born 1745, died 1815. [Howff gravestone, Dundee]

ROBERTSON, SUSAN, was accused of uttering base coin in Almerie Close, Arbroath, in 1824. [NRRS.AD14.24.107]

ROBERTSON, THOMAS, a fresh or green man aboard the Dorothy of Dundee bound for the Davis Straits in 1825. [NRS.E508.130.8]

ROBERTSON, WILLIAM, son of William Robertson, a merchant in Forfar, settled in Petersburg, Virginia before 1816, a deed. [NRS.RD5.187.241; S/H.1818]; grandson and heir of James Mudie, a merchant in Arbroath, in 1806, [NRS.S/H]; nephew and heir of David Robertson a merchant in Arbroath, appointed Thomas Robertson, a writer in Edinburgh, as his attorney in 1817. [NRS.RD5.187.241; NRS.S/H]

ROBIE, DAVID, miller in Cortachy, 1836. [NRS.GD16.28.471]

ROGER, A., master of the Prince Albert of Arbroath from Thurso to Quebec in 1849. [QM]

ROGER, CHARLES, born 1731, a manufacturer in Dundee, died 1799, husband of Katherine Young, [Howff gravestone, Dundee]

ROGER, ROBERT, and his wife Agnes Brown, parents of Charles Brown Roger, born 1854, died in Leadville, Colorado, on 24 February 1901. [Liff gravestone] [NRS.SC70.1.407/766]

ROLLAND, ALEXANDER, second son of Patrick Rolland in Montrose, died in Jamaica on 22 January 1820. [EEC.17004]

ROLLAND, JOHN, of Auchmithie, a Captain of the 3$^{rd}$ Regiment of Foot, died in Port MacQuarrie, New South Wales, Australia, on 10 November 1824. [AJ.4040]

ROLLAND, PATRICK, born 1798, son of Patrick Rolland in Montrose, a student at Marischal College, Aberdeen, in 1810, died in Jamaica on 22 January 1820. [MC.28][BM.7.463][MCA]

ROLLO, DAVID, a shipmaster in Dundee, testament, 1800, Comm. Brechin. [NRS]

RONEY, ALEXANDER, born 1827, son of John Roney and his wife Mary Law, died in Kingston, Jamaica, on 11 June 1853. [Dundee, Western gravestone]

ROSE, ALEXANDER, a surgeon from Dundee, settled in Berbice, husband of Ann Sime, testament, 1804, Comm. Edinburgh. [NRS]

ROSE, Mrs ELIZABETH, born 1777, died 12 May 1857, mother of Jane Ramsay Rose born 1814, died 29 September 1849, and Helen Rose born 1812, died at sea on 27 August 1846. [Barry gravestone]

ROSIE, WILLIAM, born 1808, a cooper who emigrated from Dundee on the brig Sprightly bound for Charleston, South Carolina, landed there in May 1828. [NARA]

ROSS, ALEXANDER, born 1752, master of the Dundee Packet in 1796, [NRS.CE1.8/47], and of the Lord Kinnear of Dundee in 1809, [DD], died in 1817. [Howff gravestone, Dundee]

ROSS, CHARLES, born 1750, a merchant in Dundee, died 1826, husband of [1] Elisabeth Clark, born 1764, died 1809, [2] Jean Mitchell, born 1772, died 1846. [Howff gravestone, Dundee]

ROSS, DAVID, a weaver, was admitted as a burgess of Arbroath in 1797. [AA.18.941]

ROSS, DAVID, born 1788, son of John Ross, a cooper in Dundee, and his wife Jean Lindsay, [1749-1821], died in New York on 29 January 1818. [Howff gravestone, Dundee]

ROSS, HERCULES, at the Cape of Good Hope, South Africa, was admitted as a burgess of Montrose in 1801. [MBR]

ROSS, HERCULES, of Rossie, versus Reverend Alexander Carnegie in Inverkeiller, 1809. [NRS.CS237.R6.29]

ROSS, HUGH, a tailor in Overgait, Dundee, was accused of mobbing and rioting in the New Hall, Bell Street, Dundee, in 1842. [NRS.AD14.42.354; JC26.1843.443]

ROSS, JAMES, graduated MA in 1803 and in 1818 a Doctor of Laws degree, a schoolmaster in Hobart, Tasmania, Australia. [MCA]

ROSS, ROBERT, a weaver, was admitted as a burgess of Arbroath in 1797. [AA.18.941]

ROSS, ROBERT, from Brechin, graduated MA from King's College, Aberdeen, in March 1840. [KCA]

ROSS, THOMAS, a merchant in Montrose, trading with Riga, Latvia, sederunt book, 1819-1820. [NRS.CS96.819]

ROSS, THOMAS, a sailor of the Friendship of Dundee at the Davis Straits in 1824. [NRS.E508.130.8]

ROSS, WILLIAM, from Brechin, graduated MA from King's College, Aberdeen, in March 1852. [KCA]

ROY, ANDREW, a journeyman wright, a lodger, was jointly accused of the murder by poison of Jean Wishart in High Street, Arbroath, in 1827. [NRS.AD14.27.179]

RUSSEL, M., sailor aboard the Princess Charlotte of Dundee bound for the Davis Strait in 1824. [NRS.E508.129.8]

RUXTON, JAMES, a weaver, was admitted as a burgess of Arbroath in 1797. [AA.18.941]

RUXTON, JOHN, a weaver, was admitted as a burgess of Arbroath in 1797. [AA.18.941]

RUXTON, ROBERT, born 1747, son of Robert Ruxton in Cairnhill, Esslemont, married Margaret Brown in Cononsyth, Carmyllie, on 5 November 1780, emigrated to America in 1788, died there in 1828. [BLG.2898]

RUXTON, ROBERT, a weaver, was admitted as a burgess of Arbroath in 1798. [AA.18.941]

RUXTON, ROBERT, formerly a sailor on a man'o'war later a tailor in Montrose, was accused of mobbing and rioting there in 1813. [NRS.AD14.13.84]

SADDLER, ELISABETH, born 1790, wife of John Lowson in Craichie, Dunnichen, was buried at Monikie on 5 July 1845. [Monikie Burial Register]

SALMOND, DAVID, master of the Nymph of Dundee in 1809. [DD]

SALMOND, GEORGE, born 1783 in Angus, died in Charleston, South Carolina, on 6 October 1838. [Old Scots gravestone, Charleston]

SALTER, THOMAS, harpooner of the Friendship of Dundee at the Davis Straits in 1824. [NRS.E508.130.8]

SANDEMAN, WILLIAM, a merchant in Dundee, also a bleacher at the Douglas Bleachfield in 1799. [DCA.B19.3.27/185-190]

SAUNDERS, ALEXANDER, master of the Bamburgh Castle of Dundee in 1809. [DD]

SAUNDERS, JAMES, the proprietor and publisher of the Dundee, Perth, and Coupar Advertiser, was accused of sedition in 1820. [NRS.AD14.20.178]

SAUNDERS, JAMES, a fresh or greenman aboard the Dorothy of Dundee bound for the Davis Straits in 1825. [NRS.E508.130.8]

SCHOLLAY, DAVID, and his wife Jane Simpson, parents of Hellen Paris Schollay, born 1856, died in Denver, Colorado, on 17 October 1899. [Arbroath Abbey gravestone]

SCOTT, ALEXANDER, a wright, was admitted as a burgess of Arbroath in 1797. [AA.18.941]

SCOTT, ALEXANDER, born 1766, a brewer and ale-seller, was admitted as a burgess of Arbroath in 1797, died 27 November 1813, husband of Helen Mill, born 1776, died 1842. [Arbroath Abbey gravestone] [AA.18.941]

SCOTT, ALEXANDER, born in July 1821 in Dundee, emigrated to New York in 1841, settled in Greenville, South Carolina. [Greenville County Records]

SCOTT, CHARLES, a weaver, was admitted as a burgess of Arbroath in 1797. [AA.18.941]

SCOTT, DAVID, the younger of Newton, married Margaret Gleig, daughter of Reverend George Gleig, in Arbroath on 2 June 1820. [SM.86.94]

SCOTT, DAVID, line manager aboard the Princess Charlotte of Dundee bound for the Davis Strait in 1824. [NRS.E508.129.8]

SCOTT, DAVID, apprentice aboard the Estridge of Dundee bound for the Davis Straits in 1824. [NRS.E508.129.8]

SCOTT, DAVID, a draper in Arbroath, was granted a tack in Arbirlot in 1841. [NRS.GD45.16.1733]

SCOTT, DUNCAN GORDON, born 5 December 1788 in Auchterhouse, son of Reverend James Scott and his wife Margaret Munro, to India in 1805, a Lieutenant General of the Bengal Army, died in Roxburghshire in April 1863. [BA.4.31]

SCOTT, GEORGE. from Forfar, graduated MA from King's College, Aberdeen, on 29 March 1811. [KCA]

SCOTT, JAMES, born 1751, a mason on Hawkhill, Dundee, died 1807, husband of Janet Bell, born 1764, died 1800. [Howff gravestone, Dundee]

SCOTT, JAMES, a weaver, was admitted as a burgess of Arbroath in 1798. [AA.18.941]

SCOTT, JAMES, born 1746, a merchant in Dundee, died in 1823, husband of Elizabeth Stewart, born 1744, died 1808. [Howff gravestone, Dundee]

SCOTT, JAMES, born 6 June 1786 in Dundee, third son of Reverend James Scott and his wife Margaret Munro in Auchterhouse, a planter at Leogane, St James, Jamaica, a witness in 1818, died in Falmouth, Jamaica, on 22 December 1824. [NRS.RD5.144.504] [EEC.17695] [F.5.310][BM.17.638]

SCOTT, JAMES, master of the Hind of Dundee in 1824, and the George of Dundee in 1825, [DSR], testament, 1837, [NRS.SC45.31.3.488]

SCOTT, JEAN, daughter of Lieutenant General James Scott of Commiston, testament, 1799, Comm. Brechin. [NRS]

SCOTT, JEAN, born 1833, wife of William Taylor, died in San Francisco, California, on 7 June 1891. [Episcopalian church, Montrose]

SCOTT, JOHN, born 1770, a shipmaster in Montrose, died 1830. [Craig Inchbrioch gravestone]

SCOTT, JOHN, sailor aboard the Princess Charlotte of Dundee bound for the Davis Straits in 1824. [NRS.E508.129.8]

SCOTT, JOHN, sailor aboard the Estridge of Dundee bound for the Davis Straits in 1824. [NRS.E508.129.8]

SCOTT, JOHN, a flax dresser in Overgait, Dundee, was accused of mobbing and rioting in the New Hall, Bell Street, Dundee, in 1842. [NRS.AD14.42.354; JC26.1843.443]

SCOTT, MARGARET, born 1764, widow of James Butter in Barry, was buried in Monikie on 8 December 1847. [Monikie Burial Register]

SCOTT, ROBERT, of Logie, born 1725 in Montrose, died in 1797, husband of Ann Ouchterlony, born 1761, died in 1824. [Montrose gravestone] [NRS.E504.E266.3.19]

SCOTT, ROBERT, born 1801, on Barry Links, died 7 August 1886, husband of Betsy Whitton, born 1808, died 27 September 1894. [Barry gravestone]

SCOTT, ROBERT, a clerk from Dundee, settled in St Mary's County, Maryland. [MSA.Wills.20.836]

SCOTT, WILLIAM, born 1736, late of the Royal Navy, later in Montrose, died in 1795, husband of Janet Scott, born 1751, died 1832, testament, 1796, Comm. Brechin. [NRS]

SCOTT, WILLIAM MERCER, fourth son of Reverend James Scott in Auchterhouse, died in Jamaica on 19 February 1820. [BM.7.343]

SCOTT, WILLIAM, a jeweller in Dundee, testament, 1800, Comm. Brechin. [NRS]

SCRYMGEOUR, HENRY, late of Jamaica, youngest son of David Scrymgeour of Birkhill, 1793. [NRS.NRAS.783/9]

SCRYMGER, JOHN, a merchant in Kirriemuir, was accused of forgery in 1832. [NRS.AD14.32.27]

SCRYMGEOUR, ROBERT, son of James Scrymgeour a shoemaker in the parish of Mains and Strathmartin, a student at Marischal College, Aberdeen, in 1845. [MCA]

SCRIMGEOUR, THOMAS, a wright in Guthrie, testaments, 1793-1794, Comm. Brechin. [NRS]

SELLAR, DAVID, a planter in Tobago, appointed Alexander Robb in Dundee, James Nicoll jr. there, and William Sellar there, as his executors in 1810. [NRS.RD3.336.135]

SHAND, CHARLES, born 1744, a merchant in Montrose, died 1795, husband of Elizabeth Mitchell who died in 1830, testament, 1795, Comm. Brechin. [NRS] [Montrose gravestone]

SHAND, GEORGE, a merchant in Montrose, was accused of mobbing and rioting there in 1813. [NRS.AD14.13.84]

SHAND, WILLIAM, a shoemaker, was admitted as a burgess of Arbroath in 1791. [AA.18.941]

SHANKS, THOMAS, a weaver, was admitted as a burgess of Arbroath in 1798. [AA.18.941]

SHANKS, WILLIAM, harpooner aboard the <u>Estridge of Dundee</u> bound for the Davis Straits in 1824. [NRS.E508.129.8]

SHARP, JAMES, born 1790 in Dundee, son of William Sharp and his wife Isabella Kinnear, died in New Orleans, Louisiana, on 13 August 1829. [Howff gravestone, Dundee]

SHARP, JAMES, sailor aboard the Estridge of Dundee bound for the Davis Straits in 1824. [NRS.E508.129.8]

SHARP, JOHN, sailor aboard the Estridge of Dundee bound for the Davis Straits in 1824. [NRS.E508.129.8]

SHARPY, HENRY, in Arbroath in 1799. [NRS.GD45.18.2012]

SHAW, DUNCAN, in Milton of Cortachy, testaments, 1779 and 1796, Comm. Brechin. [NRS]

SHAW, DUNCAN, born 1768 in Angus, settled in New Brunswick, in 1790, died in Hillsborough, N.B., on 3 May 1843. [New Brunswick Courier, 20.5.1843]

SHAW, JOHN, at Scouringburn Dundee, was accused of theft in the parish of Mains and Strathmartine in 1822. [NRS.AD14.22.67]

SHEPHERD, GEORGE, and his wife Isabel Middleton, parents of John Munro Shepherd, born 1853, who died in Missuala, Montana, on 18 September 1902. [Rosehill gravestone, Montrose]

SHEPHERD, JAMES, a seaman in Auchmithie around 1796. [St Vigeans gravestone]

SHEPHERD, JAMES, a merchant in Kirriemuir, died 1809, ledgers, 1785-1807. [NRS.CS96.1910]

SHEPHERD, MUNGO, a merchant in Dundee in 1798. [DCA.B19.3.27/13]

SHERRIFS, GEORGE, son of David Sherrifs in Inverkeilor, graduated MA from Marischal College, Aberdeen, in 1820, later a schoolmaster in Kirkden. [MCA]

SHERIFF, GEORGE, a tailor at Gallow Law, Panbride, a tack, 1840. [NRS.GD45.16]

SHIEL, GEORGE, master of the <u>Thomas and Ann of Arbroath</u> trading between Riga, Latvia, and Dundee in 1819. [NRS.E504.11.21]

SHIELD, WILLIAM, a blacksmith in Arbirlot, 1846. [NRS.GD45.16.1735]

SHORT, THOMAS, a founder in Arbroath, accused of theft in 1812. [NRS.AD14.12.8]

SIBBALD, MARY W., born 1825, daughter of David Sibbald and his wife Anne, died in California on 8 November 1853. [St Peter's gravestone, Dundee]

SIEVEWRIGHT, COLIN, a medical student in Brechin, a witness to a deed of James Lowe a sugar planter in Trinidad in 1809. [NRS.RD3.315.571]

SIEVEWRIGHT, DAVID, born in Brechin, a hawker, was accused of housebreaking and theft at Northgate, Noranside, Fearn, in 1831. [NRS.AD14.31.19]

SIEVWRIGHT, ROBERT, born 1743, a shipmaster burgess of Dundee in 1796, died in 1807, husband of Christian Thain, born 1755, died 1788. [DBR][Howff gravestone, Dundee]

SIM, JAMES MILN, Ensign of the 1st Battalion, 11th Regiment, Bengal Native Infantry, son of Reverend David Sim minister of Barry, 1811. [NRS.GD51.4.512]

SIM, JOHN, a weaver, was admitted as a burgess of Arbroath in 1797. [AA.18.941]

SIM, ROBERT, a tenant in Newton Arbirlot, versus Margaret Miles, a decreet of divorce, 1837. [NRS.CS46.1837.12.18]

SIM, WILLIAM, in Arbroath, son of Robert Sim tenant in Bandoch, a Precept of Removal, 1815. [NRS.GD45.18.2358]

SIME ALEXANDER, born in 1839, son of William Sime, died in Lambayeque, Peru, on 20 May 1901. [Western gravestone, Dundee]

SIME, CRAWFORD, son of William Sime, [1797-1863], died in Rio de Janeiro, Brazil, aged 21. [Western gravestone, Dundee]

SIME, JAMES, master of the Aurora of Dundee when bound from Riga, Latvia, to Lisbon, Portugal, was captured by a French privateer in 1798. [AJ.665]

SIME, WILLIAM, a wright in Dundee, a letter to Provost John Caw of Perth in 1803. [PKA.B59.25.3.179]

SYMMERS, COLIN, Customs Collector at the Port of Dundee in 1820. [NRS.E504.11.21]

SYMMERS, JOHN and GEORGE, exported a cargo of rum from Dundee aboard the Psyche, Captain Erskine, bound for Quebec in April 1820. [NRS.E504.11.21]

SIMMONS, WILLIAM, master of the Dispatch of Dundee trading between London and Dundee in 1818. [NRS.E504.11.21]

SIMPSON, JAMES, from Farnell, graduated MA from King's College, Aberdeen, in March 1841. [KCA]

SIMPSON, JOHN, a carter, was admitted as a burgess of Arbroath in 1791. [AA.18.941]

SIMPSON, ROBERT, a skipper at Craig, Dundee, master of the Peggy of Dundee in 1809, [DD], of the Mary in 1818, and of the Jane of Dundee in 1824. [DSR]

SIMPSON, ROBERT, from Angus, graduated MA from King's College, Aberdeen, on 31 March 1831. [KCA]

SIMPSON, THOMAS, master of the Marquis of Cornwallis in 1809. [DD]

SIMPSON, WILLIAM KINNEAR, son of David Simpson in Dundee, settled in Silver City, Utah, by 1873. [NRS.S/H]

SIMPSON, ……, master of a smack of Arbroath, which was shipwrecked off Carlingford, Ireland, in 1799. [AJ.2669]

SINCLAIR, Captain, master of the British King of Dundee from Dundee to Riga, Latvia, in 1844. [MD.160]

SKEEN, JOHN, born 1795 in Angus, a tailor, emigrated via Dundee to America, was naturalised in New York on 22 February 1820. [Court of Common Pleas, New York]

SKENE, MALCOLM, a merchant in Brechin, 1811. [NRS.CS233.SEQN.M1.76]

SKINNER, CHARLES, son of John Skinner an Episcopalian minister in Forfar, a student at Marischal College, Aberdeen, in 1820s. [MCA]

SKINNER, JAMES, son of James Skinner a weaver in Dundee a student at Marischal College, Aberdeen, in 1830s. [MCA]

SKINNER, JAMES, son of John Skinner an Episcopalian minister in Forfar, a student at Marischal College, Aberdeen, in 1832. [MCA]

SKINNER, JAMES, son of John Skinner an Episcopalian minister in Forfar, graduated MA from Marischal College, Aberdeen, in 1818. [MCA]

SKINNER, THOMAS, a fresh or green man aboard the Dorothy of Dundee bound for the Davis Straits in 1825. [NRS.E508.130.8]

SKINNER, WILLIAM, son of John Skinner an Episcopalian minister in Forfar, a student at Marischal College, Aberdeen, in 1820s, an advocate in Aberdeen in 1829. [MCA]

SMALL, ANDREW, born 1753, a weaver on Hawkhill, Dundee, died 1816, husband of Isabel Nicol. [Howff gravestone, Dundee]

SMALL, ANDREW, born 28 August 1794, son of Andrew Small a teacher in Lochee, emigrated to America in 1829, died in Washington, D.C., on 6 April 1847. [Darnestown, Montgomery County, gravestone]

SMALL, JAMES, third son of James Small in Montrose, died at Montego Bay, Jamaica, on 24 November 1821. [EEC.17257] [BM.11.383]

SMALL, JOHN, a weaver, was admitted as a burgess of Arbroath in 1798. [AA.18.941]

SMALL, MARY, daughter of James Small, married John Linnell of Burret Pen, Hanover, Jamaica, at Montego Bay, Jamaica, on 24 November 1821. [AJ.4871]

SMALL, ROBERT, eldest son of James Small in Montrose, died at Flamstead, Montego Bay, Jamaica, on 16 October 1821. [BM.11.383]

SMALL, WILLIAM, a writer in Dundee in 1798, husband of Jean Davidson, born 1717, died 1782. [DCA.B19.3.27/8] [Howff gravestone, Dundee]

SMART, DAVID, born 1731, a baker in Dundee, died 1806. [Howff gravestone, Dundee]

SMART, JAMES, born 1747, a baker in Dundee, died 1798, husband of Ann Norval, born 1759, died 1834. [Howff gravestone, Dundee]

SMART, JOHN, in Auchire, a Precept of Removal, 1815. [NRS.GD45.18.2358]

SMART, THOMAS, born 1726, a mason, architect, burgess and guilds-brother of Dundee, died 1801, husband of Mary Ogilvie, born 1719, died 1799. [Howff gravestone, Dundee]

SMITH, ALEXANDER, born 1729, died 1802, husband of Helen Baillie, born 1733, died 1802. [Howff gravestone, Dundee]

SMITH, ALEXANDER, master of the Hind of Dundee trading between St John, New Brunswick, New York and Dundee in 1820, 1819. [NRS.E504.11.21]

SMITH, ARCHIBALD, born 1712, died in 1797, husband of Janet Ogilvie, born 1726, died in 1796. [Montrose gravestone]

SMITH, CHARLES, born in Dundee, 'died at an advanced age' in New York in 1813. [EA.5163.13]

SMITH, CHARLES an apprentice aboard the Friendship of Dundee at the Davis Straits in 1824. [NRS.E508.130.8] [DSR]

SMITH, GEORGE, born 1740, a tailor in Dundee, died 1804, husband of Catherine Thomson. [Howff gravestone, Dundee]

SMITH, JAMES, a shoemaker, was admitted as a burgess of Arbroath in 1791. [AA.18.941]

SMITH, JAMES, born 1724, a gardener at Chapelshade, Dundee, died 1813, husband of Janet Slater, born 1752, died 1804. [Howff gravestone, Dundee]

SMITH, JAMES, the Bank of Scotland agent in Brechin, sederunt books, 1805-1824. [NRS.CS96.1259]

SMITH, JAMES, from Angus, graduated MA from King's College, Aberdeen, on 26 April 1813, later in the Service of the East India Company. [KCA]

SMITH, JAMES, apprentice aboard the Estridge of Dundee, bound for the Davis Straits in 1824. [NRS.E508.129.8]

SMITH, JAMES, steersman aboard the Estridge of Dundee, bound for the Davis Straits in 1824. [NRS.E508.129.8]

SMITH, JAMES, born 1818, died in Melbourne, Australia, on 21 June 1895. [Western gravestone, Dundee]

SMITH, JAMES, born 1818, died 1895, father of William Smith, born 1851, died in Melbourne, Australia, on 10 February 1888. [Western gravestone, Dundee]

SMITH, JOHN, first son of George Smith, farmer of Bogside, Tannadice, born there, and his wife Agnes, daughter of William Candy farmer in Newbiggin, born in Cortachy, was born on 21 February 1809, and baptised in the Qualified Episcopal Chapel in Dundee on 8 April 1809. [DE.75]

SMITH, JOHN, a weaver, was admitted as a burgess of Arbroath in 1797. [AA.18.941]

SMITH, JOHN, a weaver in Lawson's Close, Overgait, Dundee, accused of armed robbery in 1840. [NRS.AD14.40.295]

SMITH, MARIA, born 1843, daughter of Alexander Smith and his wife Barbara Guthrie, died in San Francisco, California, on 12 September 1882. [Arbroath gravestone]

SMITH, PATRICK, a bailie of Dundee in 1798. [DCA.B19.3.27/1]

SMITH, PETER, born at Dickmontlaw near Montrose, a mariner aboard the schooner Jean, was accused of murder and piracy in 1821. [NRS.AD14.21.38]

SMITH, PETER, steersman aboard the Dorothy of Dundee bound for the Davis Straits in 1825. [NRS.E508.130.8]

SMITH, PETER, from Brechin, settled in Andover, Massachusetts, by 1878. [NRS.NRAS.2182]

SMITH, ROBERT, a flax-dresser, was admitted as a burgess of Arbroath in 1797. [AA.18.941]

SMITH, ROBERT, a sawyer in Drumgeith, victim of an armed robbery in 1840. [NRS.AD14.40.295]

SMITH, THOMAS, a merchant, was admitted as a burgess of Arbroath in 1797. [AA.18.941]; born 1743, died 4 February 1813, husband of Jean Gardner, born 1742, died 1796. [Arbroath Abbey gravestone]

SMITH, THOMAS, a flax-dresser, was admitted as a burgess of Arbroath in 1798. [AA.18.941]

SMITH, WILLIAM, born 1737, a weaver in Montrose, died 1806. [Montrose gravestone]

SMITH, WILLIAM, a blacksmith, was admitted as a burgess of Arbroath in 1795. [AA.18.941]

SMITH, WILLIAM, sr. from Forfar, graduated MA from King's College, Aberdeen, on 30 March 1810. [KCA]

SMITH, WILLIAM, jr. from Forfar, graduated MA from King's College, Aberdeen, on 30 March 1810. [KCA]

SMITH, WILLIAM, a skipper in Castle Court, Dundee, master of the Glenalmond in 1818. [DD]

SMITH, WILLIAM, was born in Stonehaven, Kincardineshire, a weaver in Forfar, Angus, was accused of theft in Letham, Angus, in 1822. [NRS.AD14.22.56]

SMITH, WILLIAM, son of William Smith an architect in Montrose, graduated MA from Marischal College, Aberdeen, in 1832. [MCA]

SMITH, WILLIAM, a vintner, was granted a tack in Edzell, in 1843. [NRS.GD45.16.1930]

SMITH, WILLIAM BERRY, youngest son of Captain John Smith of the Forfar and Kincardineshire Militia, died in Sofala, New South Wales, Australia, on 9 September 1855. [AJ.5636]

SMYTH, JAMES, a weaver, was admitted as a burgess of Arbroath in 1797. [AA.18.941]

SMYTH, JEAN, widow of David Greig feuar in the Nether Tenements of Caldhame, testament, 1794, Comm. Brechin. [NRS]

SMYTH, JOHN, Provost of Brechin, testament, 1800, Comm. Brechin. [NRS]

SMYTH, RALPH, a tenant in Pitlivie, testament, 1796, Comm. Brechin. [NRS]

SOMERVILLE, JAMES, from Angus, graduated MA from King's College, Aberdeen, on 27 March 1796. [KCA]

SOOT, THOMAS, sailor aboard the Princess Charlotte of Dundee bound for the Davis Strait in 1824. [NRS.E508.129.8]

SORREL, JOHN, born 1769, died in 1828. [Maryton gravestone]

SOUTAR, BELL, was accused of housebreaking and theft at the Swan Inn, Brechin, in 1830. [NRS.JC26.1830.18]

SOUTAR, JAMES, a manufacturer in Dundee in 1796. [DCA.B19.3.27/1]

SOUTAR, JOHN, a cabinetmaker, was admitted as a burgess of Arbroath in 1795. [AA.18.941]

SOUTAR, JOHN, a merchant, was admitted as a burgess of Arbroath in 1795. [AA.18.941]

SOUTTER, ROBERT, from Dundee, and his wife Margaret Taylor, from Forfar, settled in Norfolk, Virginia, before 1810. [ANY]

SOUTTER, WILLIAM, probably from Angus, died in California on 21 November 1863. [NRS.S/H.1856/1873]

SPALDING, JAMES, born 1771, a skipper in Tindall's Wynd, Dundee, master of the Tay of Dundee in 1809, and the Newcastle and Berwick Packet in 1818, also the Mary of Dundee in 1824, died 1836, testament, 1837. [NRS.SC45.31.3.403] [DSR]

SPEID, JAMES, once a merchant, later a land-waiter in Dundee, testament, 1791, Comm. Brechin. [NRS]

SPEID, THOMAS, a shoemaker in Dundee, testament, 1792, Comm. Brechin. [NRS]

SPENS, ISOBEL, widow of David Allardyce a merchant in Brechin, testament 1797, Comm. Brechin. [NRS]

SPENS, JOHN, late Commissary of Brechin, testament, 1791, Comm. Brechin. [NRS]

SPENCE, JOHN, the factor for the lordship of Brechin, feus of Caldhame, and the baronies of Lochee, Edzell, Navar and Lethnott, records 1784-1801. [NRS.GD45.18.1749-1763]

SPENS, WILLIAM, a merchant in Dundee, testament, 1799, Comm. Brechin. [NRS]

SPINK, DAVID, born 1774, a seaman in Auchmithie, died in 1814. [St Vigean's gravestone]

SPINK, JAMES, born 1761, a shipmaster in Arbroath who was drowned off Lerwick, Shetland Islands, in 1803. [Arbroath Abbey gravestone]

SPINK, JAMES, born 1800 in Arbroath, settled in Darien, Georgia, died in Savanna, Georgia, on 16 November 1823. [Daily Georgian, 21.11.1822]

SPINK, JAMES, born 1801, a fisherman, died 19 July 1848, husband of Isobel Swankie, born 1801, died 6 July 1865. [St Vigeans gravestone]

SPINK, JOHN, a shipmaster in Arbroath, testament, 1803, Comm. St Andrews. [NRS]

SPINK, ROBERT, a skipper in Barrack Street, Dundee, master of the Osnaburgh in 1818, and the Dundee of Dundee in 1824. [DSR]

SPRUNT, WILLIAM, a cloth lapper in Maxwelltown Street, Dundee, victim of an armed robbery in 1840. [NRS.AD14.40.295]

STEILL, DAVID, of the Friendship of Dundee at the Davis Straits in 1824. [NRS.E508.130.8]

STEEL, MARY, in Almerie Close, Arbroath, was accused of assaulting Margaret Hall in 1818. [NRS.AD14.18.87]

STEPHENS, J., from Montrose, father of William W. Stephens in Spring Valley, who married Elizabeth Peddie, only daughter of John Peddie in Montrose, in the International Hotel, Toano, Nevada, on 16 December 1873. [S.9503]

STEPHENS, MARGARET, born 1728, died 1816. [Howff gravestone, Dundee]

STEPHENS, ROBERT, printer of the Dundee, Perth, and Coupar Advertiser, was accused of sedition in 1820. [NRS.AD14.20.178]

STEPHEN, WILLIAM, born 1734, a wright in Dundee, died 1820, husband of Alison Mitchell, born 1743, died 1801. [Howff gravestone, Dundee]

STEPHENSON, DAVID, a sailor aboard the whaler Mary Ann of Dundee from Dundee to Greenland on 4 March 1813, abandoned the ship on return at Aberdeen to avoid the Press Gang on 16 August 1813. [NRS.E508.115.8]

STEPHENSON, THOMAS, in Chapelton, Kirriemuir, a victim of forgery in 1832. [NRS.AD14.32.27]

STEVENS, ROBERT, a weaver in Monifieth, a tack, 1840. [NRS.GD45.1.2069]

STEVENSON, JAMES, a hay-dresser, was admitted as a burgess of Arbroath in 1797. [AA.18.941]

STEVENSON, JOHN, son of Thomas Stevenson MD in Arbroath, a student in Marischal College in 1790s. [MCA]

STEVENSON, JOHN, harpooner aboard the Estridge of Dundee bound for the Davis Straits in 1824. [NRS.E508.129.8]

STEVENSON, THOMAS, MD, born 1761, died 1799, husband of Ann Adam, born 1761, died in 1847. [Arbroath Abbey gravestone]

STEWART, ALEXANDER, born 1818, son of Walter Stewart and his wife Mary Hill, died at Colorado Springs, Colorado, on 17 April 1884. [Forfar gravestone]

STEWART, CHARLES, born in Airlie on 3 August 1783, son of John Stewart and his wife Isabel Ellis, married Isabella ...., parents of John Stewart born 1810, a farmer who was naturalised in New York on 2 October 1819. [N.Y. Court of Common Pleas]

STEWART, DANIEL, a weaver in Glencoe Park, Forfar, was accused of housebreaking at Balgavies, Aberlemno, in 1830. [NRS.AD14.30.56; JC26.1830.16]

STEWART, DAVID, a porter, husband of [1] Barbara Allan, born 1754, died 1809, [2] Alison Farquhar. [Howff gravestone, Dundee]

STEWART, DAVID, harpooner of the Friendship of Dundee at the Davis Straits in 1824. [NRS.E508.130.8]

STEWART, ELIZABETH, daughter of James Stewart in Montrose, married John Thomson, in Jersey City, New Jersey, on 8 December 1870. [S.8556]

STEWART, GEORGE, a weaver, was admitted as a burgess of Arbroath in 1797. [AA.18.941]

STEWART, JAMES, a skinner, was admitted as a burgess of Arbroath in 1791. [AA.18.941]

STEWART, JAMES, from Arbroath, of the Royal Navy, testament, 1807, testament, St Andrews. [NRS]

STEWART, JAMES, born 1740, a surgeon, died 1821. [Howff gravestone, Dundee]

STEWART, JOHN, son of Thomas Stewart the town clerk of Montrose, a student in Marischal College in 1790s. [MCA]

STEWART, Mrs MARGARET, wife of David Stewart a sailor, in King Street, Dundee, the victim of an assault in 1847. [NRS.AD14.47.71]

STEWART, PETER, a labourer in Cloisterbank, Kirriemuir, was accused of assault and murder in 1831. [NRS.AD14.31.18]

STEWART, THOMAS, a weaver in the factory of Thomas Webster and Company, Hawkhill, Dundee, was accused of mobbing and rioting in 1816. [NRS.AD14.16.58]

STEWART, WILLIAM, in Cairnleith, Kingoldrum, testament, 1798, Comm. Brechin. [NRS]

STEWART, WILLIAM, born 1785, farmer at Dalbrack, died 3 November 1853, husband of Mary Grant, born 1798, died at Glen Tennet on 5 August 1875. [Lochlee gravestone]

STILL, JAMES, a saddler, was admitted as a burgess of Arbroath in 1797. [AA.18.941]

STILLER, WILLIAM, a weaver, was admitted as a burgess of Arbroath in 1797. [AA.18.941]

STINSON, ……, line manager aboard the Dorothy of Dundee bound for the Davis Straits in 1825. [NRS.E508.130.8]

STIRLING, JAMES, in South Muir, Forfar, was accused of theft in 1825. [NRS.AD14.25.244]

STIRLING, JAMES, born 1819, married, a carter in Stobswell, Dundee, was accused of assault in 1847. [NRS.AD14.47.71]

STIVAN, GEORGE, a weaver, was admitted as a burgess of Arbroath in 1797. [AA.18.941]

STIVAN, JOHN, a shoemaker, was admitted as a burgess of Arbroath in 1797. [AA.18.941]

STIVEN, WILLIAM, born 1775, a shipmaster in Arbroath, died at sea in 1823, husband of Margaret Air. [Arbroath Abbey gravestone]

STORMONTH, ALEXANDER, in Broughty Ferry, a victim of theft in 1824. [NRS.AD14.24.95]

STORMONTH, JAMES, son of Alexander Stormonth MD in Broughty Ferry, a student at Marischal College, Aberdeen in 1830s. [MCA]

STORRIER, ROBERT, a weaver, was admitted as a burgess of Arbroath in 1797. [AA.18.941]

STRACHAN, ANDREW, a shipmaster in Montrose, testament, 1798, Comm. Brechin. [NRS]

STRACHAN, CHARLES, and his wife Elizabeth Smart, [1750-1831], parents of Charles Strachan on Southampton Island, Jamaica. [Edzell gravestone]

STRACHAN, JAMES, born 1769, died in 1810, husband of Mary Cobb, born 1757, died in 1800. [Montrose gravestone]

STRACHAN, JAMES, son of William Strachan and his wife Ann Tyler, died in Jamaica on 4 March 1841. [Arbroath Abbey gravestone]

STRACHAN, JAMES, from Montrose, died in the USA, father of George Blair Strachan, probate June 1844, PCC. [TNA]

STRACHAN, JOHN, born 1762, a shipmaster of Arbroath, died in 1830. [Arbroath Abbey gravestone]

STRACHAN, JOHN, a weaver, was admitted as a burgess of Arbroath in 1797. [AA.18.941]

STRACHAN, JOHN, born 1770, a merchant in Montrose, died 1823, father of James Ford Strachan a member of the Legislative Council of Victoria, Australia. [Montrose Episcopal gravestone]

STRACHAN, ROBERT, harpooner aboard the <u>Estridge of Dundee,</u> bound for the Davis Straits in 1824. [NRS.E508.129.8]

STRACHAN, WILLIAM, a sawyer, was admitted as a burgess of Arbroath in 1797. [AA.18.941]

STRACHAN, WILLIAM, master of the Hero of Dundee in 1809. [DD]

STRACHAN, WILLIAM, son of James Strachan a merchant in Brechin, a student at Marischal College, Aberdeen, in 1820s. [MCA]

STRACHAN, WILLIAM DOVERTIE, from Forfar, graduated MA from King's College, Aberdeen, in March 1826. [KCA]

STRANG, JAMES, in Wellbraehead, Forfar, a victim of theft in 1825. [NRS.AD14.25.244]

STRANG, JOHN, a weaver in Sparrowcroft, Forfar, a victim of theft in 1825. [NRS.AD14.25.244]

STRANG, WILLIAM, minister of the Relief Congregation in the Seagait, Dundee, in 1820. [NRS.CS271.68562]

STRATHERN, PETER, versus the Dundee and Newtyle Railway Company in 1844. [NRS.CS311.1337]

STRATON, ELIZABETH, born 1734, daughter of John Straton of Lauriston, died in Montrose on 20 July 1820. [SM.86.192]

STRATON, JEAN, born 1735, daughter of Patrick Straton, died in Montrose on 16 May 1823. [SM.86.96]

STRATON, WILLIAM, son of Alexander Straton in Dundee, a student at Marischal College around 1817. [MCA]

STRATTON, ISABEL, born 1759, died 1790, wife of James Martin. [Howff gravestone, Dundee]

STREIBER, AUGUSTUS, was admitted as a burgess of Arbroath in 1790. [AA.18.941]

STUART, JOHN ALEXANDER, son of John Stuart, a Sergeant of the 2nd Battalion of the 79th Regiment of Foot, and his wife Esther, was born on 22 September 1813, and baptised in the Scottish Episcopal Church in Dundee on 10 October 1813. [DE.79]

STURROCK, ALEXANDER, a weaver, was admitted as a burgess of Arbroath in 1797. [AA.18.941]

STURROCK, DAVID, born 1799, master of the Heroine, died 29 March 1854. [HS.18.1.17] [DD] [Howff gravestone, Dundee]

STURROCK, JAMES, master of the Alexander of Dundee, bound from Dundee for New York in January 1819, [NRS.E504.11.21]; 1853. [DD] [HS.18.1.17]

STURROCK, JOHN, was admitted as a burgess of Arbroath in 1797. [AA.18.941]

STURROCK, JOHN, a gardener at the Hatton, Panbride, a tack, 1840. [NRS.GD45.16]

STURROCK, ROBERT, born 1769, farmer at West Stotefaulds, was buried in Monikie on 24 May 1844. [Monikie Burial Register]

STURROCK, PETER, a merchant, was admitted as a burgess of Arbroath in 1797. [AA.18.941]

SUTHERLAND, JOHN, a messenger-at-arms, in Forfar, 1825. [NRS.AD14.25.83]

SWORD, ANDREW, master of the Perseverance of Dundee and of the Peggy of Dundee in 1825. [DSR]

SWORD, THOMAS, sailor aboard the Princess Charlotte of Dundee bound for the Davis Strait in 1824. [NRS.E508.129.8]

SYME, JOHN, a surgeon in Dundee, testament, 1795, Comm. Brechin. [NRS]

TAINSH, JOHN, in West Ferry, a salmon fisher, a Precept of Removal, 1815. [NRS.GD45.18.2358]

TAIT, HUGH, an apprentice aboard the Dorothy of Dundee bound for the Davis Straits in 1825. [NRS.E508.130.8]

TARBAT, ALEXANDER, son of Marjory Rose or Tarbat in Forfar, a plasterer who settled in California, later in New York, a sasine, 1857. [NRS.RS.Forfar.18.206; NRS.S/H]

TASKER, DAVID, harpooner aboard the Dorothy of Dundee bound for the Davis Straits in 1825. [NRS.E508.130.8]

TASKER, ROBERT, a sailor aboard the Friendship of Dundee at the Davis Straits in 1824. [NRS.E508.130.8]

TAVENDALE, ALEXANDER, a weaver, was admitted as a burgess of Arbroath in 1795. [AA.18.941]

TAWES, JOHN, in North Muir, Kirriemuir, a Revenue officer, who was assaulted in Cortacht-Clova in 1824, trial papers. [NRS.JC26.1824.82]

TAYLOR, ALEXANDER, born in Brechin, a mariner who was naturalised on Charleston, South Carolina, on 22 February 1797. [NARA.M1183.1]

TAYLOR, ANDREW, born 1752, a maltman in Dundee, died 1801, husband of Elizabeth Boick. [Howff gravestone, Dundee]

TAYLOR, DAVID, in South Muir, Forfar, a victim of a mob and rioters in the New Hall, Bell Street, Dundee, in 1842. [NRS.AD14.42.354; JC26.1843.443]

TAYLOR, JOHN, master of the Nelly of Dundee trading between Memel, Lithuania, and Dundee in 1819. [NRS.E504.11.21]

TAYLOR, ROBERT, son of Reverend John Taylor in Lethnot, graduated MA from Marischal College, Aberdeen, in 1813, later a merchant in London. [MCA]

TAYLOR, WILLIAM, son of Alexander Taylor of Lunan, a student in Marischal College, Aberdeen, in 1790s. [MCA]

TAYLOR, WILLIAM, a shoemaker, was admitted as a burgess of Arbroath in 1792. [AA.18.941]

TAYLOR, WILLIAM, born 1790, son of William Taylor a merchant, emigrated to New York in 1803, died there on 23 March 1811. [Howff gravestone, Dundee]

TAYLOR, WILLIAM, master of the Vine of Dundee in 1825, and of the Branch of Dundee in 1825, [DSR]; testament, 1834. [NRS.SC45.31.2.184]

TAYLOR, Captain, master of the Selma of Dundee from Dundee to Quebec in 1846. [DPCA.2333]

TEMPLEMAN, THOMAS, a salmon fisher in West Ferry, re an assignation of land in Newton Panbride, 1840. [NRS.GD45.16.2155]

TEVIOTDALE, ALEXANDER, a weaver burgess of Arbroath in 1796, husband of Ann Williamson. [Arbroath Abbey gravestone]

THOM, ADAM, from Angus, graduated MA from King's College, Aberdeen, in March 1823. [KCA]

THOM, DAVID, a slater in Montrose, was accused of mobbing and rioting there in 1813. [NRS.AD14.13.84]

THOM, JAMES, a sawyer, was admitted as a burgess of Arbroath in 1797. [AA.18.941]

THOMS, ALEXANDER, of Rumgally, born 1730, a merchant and Provost of Dundee, died 1809, husband of Grace Wise, born 1763, died 1847. [Howff gravestone, Dundee]

THOMAS, ANDREW, a sailor aboard the Dorothy of Dundee bound for the Davis Straits in 1825. [NRS.E508.130.8]

THOMS, ALEXANDER, master of the Delight of Dundee trading between Easdale and Dundee in 1819. [NRS.E504.11.21]

THOMS, GEORGE, master of the Calypso of Dundee trading between St Petersburg and Dundee in 1819, [NRS.E504.11.21]; master of the Thomas in 1824. [DD]; master of the Victoria of Dundee from Dundee to Montreal in 1837, from Dundee to Quebec in 1838, from Leith to Montreal in 1840, from Dundee to Montreal in 1842. [DPCA][QM][MG]

THOMS, WILLIAM, master of the Fairy in 1824. [DD]

THOMSON, ALEXANDER, in Linlathen, 1805. [NRS.GD83.640]

THOMSON, CHARLES, town clerk, was admitted as a burgess of Arbroath in 1792. [AA.18.941]

THOMSON, DAVID, eldest son of David Thomson a farmer in Scotstoun, Forfar, settled in Vernon, Oneida County, New York, before 1821. [NRS.RD5.218.326]

THOMSON, DONALD, a sailor on the Dorothy of Dundee, 1818. [DD]

THOMSON, ELIZABETH, third daughter of David Thomson a farmer in Scotstoun, Forfar, wife of John Crichton a stonecutter, settled in Oneida County, New York, before 1821. [NRS.RD5.218.326]

THOMSON, JAMES, from Aberdeen, was admitted as a burgess of Arbroath in 1791. [AA.18.941]

THOMSON, JAMES, from Angus, graduated MA from King's College, Aberdeen, on 27 March 1795. [KCA]

THOMSON, JAMES, a weaver, was admitted as a burgess of Arbroath in 1797. [AA.18.941]

THOMSON, JAMES, a tailor in Arbroath, father of William Thomson who settled in Clinton, Iowa, before 1872. [NRS.S/H]

THOMSON, JOHN, a baker in Dundee in 1799. [DCA.B19.3.27/159]

THOMSON, JOHN, born 1733, a feuar in Lochee, died 1805. [Howff gravestone, Dundee]

THOMSON, JOHN, in Jamaica, later in Montrose, testament, 2 March 1814. [NRS.CC3.126]

THOMSON, THOMAS, a merchant tailor in Kirriemuir, sederunt book, 1826-1827. [NRS.CS96.3724]

THOMSON, WILLIAM, a sailor aboard the Friendship of Dundee at the Davis Straits in 1824. [NRS.E508.130.8]

THOMSON, WILLIAM, born 1780, a quarrier at Wellbank, was buried in Monikie on 23 August 1844. [Monikie Burial Register]

TODD, ALEXANDER, from Brechin, graduated MA from King's College, Aberdeen, in March 1835. [KCA]

TODD, JOHN, a skipper in Butcher Row, Dundee, in 1818, [DD], master of the Diamond of Dundee in 1809, and of the Perth in 1818, [DD], of the Augusta of Dundee in 1824, and of the Defiance of Dundee in 1825, a burgess of Dundee in 1828. [DSR][DBR]

TODD, JOHN, a journeyman carpenter, son of John Todd a shipmaster in Dundee, was accused of assault in 1819. [NRS.AD14.19.167]

TOSH, ALEXANDER, a sailor aboard the Dorothy of Dundee bound for the Davis Straits in 1825. [NRS.E508.130.8]

TOSH, CHARLES, born 1775, a skipper on Yeaman's Shore, Dundee, [DD], master of the Isabella of Dundee in 1809, and of the Myrtle of Dundee in 1818, 1825, [DD][DSR], died in 1834, testament, 1837. [NRS.SC45.31.3.434] [Howff gravestone, Dundee]

TOSH, LINDSAY, a sailor aboard the Dorothy of Dundee bound for the Davis Straits in 1825. [NRS.E508.130.8]

TOUGH, DAVID, and his wife Ann Williams, parents of David Tough, born 1860, who died in New Mexico on 9 May 1891. [Eastern Necropolis gravestone, Dundee]

TOWART, ROBERT, from Dundee, a hat manufacturer in New York, died in 1836, testament, 1839. [NRS.SC70.1.58]

TRAIL, ANTONY, son of Thomas Trail in Montrose, a student at Marischal College, Aberdeen, graduated MA in 1821, later a Writer to the Signet by 1829. [MCA]

TRAIL, JOHN, a wright, was admitted as a burgess of Arbroath in 1795. [AA.18.941]

TRAIL, ROBERT, son of Robert Trail a shoemaker in Montrose, graduated MA from Marischal College, Aberdeen, in 1837, later a Free Church minister in Boyndie. [MCA]

TURNBULL, ALEXANDER, a skipper in Couttie's Wynd, Dundee, 1818, [DD], master of the Shields Packet of Dundee in 1795. [NRS.CE70.1.8/5]

TURNBULL, THOMAS, born 1807, son of Hector Turnbull and his wife Jacobina Walker, died in Auckland, New Zealand, on 23 July 1868. [Trottick gravestone, Dundee]

TWEDALE, JOHN, a vintner and mail coach contractor in Montrose, sederunt book, 1824. [NRS.CS96.3627]

TWEEDIE, ANN, widow of Dr Charles Nisbet, formerly a minister in Montrose, President of Dickenson College, Carlisle, New Jersey, died there on 12 May 1807. [SM.70.158]

TYRIE, ISOBEL, born 1749, died 1810, wife of Alexander Scott a weaver at Blackscroft, Dundee. [Howff gravestone, Dundee]

URE, ELIZABETH, daughter of John Ure the Sheriff clerk of Angus, and wife of Reverend John Skinner, died at Inchgarth near Forfar on 12 May 1820. [SM.86.96]

URQUHART, PETER, an apprentice shipbuilder of John Calman in Dundee, was accused of mobbing ad rioting in 1816. [NRS.AD14.16.52]

VALENTINE, ALEXANDER, a merchant in Brechin, testament, 1795, Comm. Brechin. [NRS]

VALENTINE, JOHN, a tailor in Brechin, an inmate of Montrose Lunatic Asylum in 1842. [NRS.CS313.388]

VALENTINE, THOMAS W., son of David Valentine in Montrose, a student at Marischal College, Aberdeen, in 1829. [MCA]

VALENTINE, WILLIAM, master of the Horn of Dundee in 1809, and of the Achilles, in 1824. [DD]

WALKER, GEORGE, sailor aboard the Estridge of Dundee, bound for the Davis Straits in 1824. [NRS.E508.129.8]

WALKER, HARRIET, born 1808, emigrated from Dundee on the barque Herald bound for Charleston, South Carolina, landed there in October 1826. [NARA]

WALKER, JAMES, born 1736, died 1821. [Montrose gravestone]

WALKER, JAMES, a weaver, was admitted as a burgess of Arbroath in 1797. [AA.18.941]

WALKER, JAMES, from Angus, graduated MA from King's College, Aberdeen, on 26 April 1813. [KCA]

WALKER, JAMES, son of James Walker a farmer in Newbigging by Montrose, a student at Marischal College, Aberdeen, in 1814. [MCA]

WALKER, JAMES, a writer in Forfar, married Catherine Michie, daughter of William Michie of Carseburn, at Tillywhandland on 5 June 1820. [SM.86.94]

WALKER, JAMES, born 1807, a flax spinner in Dundee, died 1879. [SLH.105]

WALKER, JAMES, from Montrose, died in Jamaica, an inventory, 1826. [NRS.C70.1.34]

WALKER, JAMES, a shipwright, aged 65, died in Germantown, Australia, in 18..... [Howff gravestone, Dundee]

WALKER, JOHN, a fish cadger in Carnoustie, victim of an armed robbery in 1840. [NRS.AD14.40.295]

WALKER, ROBERT, a saddler, was admitted as a burgess of Arbroath in 1797. [AA.18.941]

WALKER, WILLIAM, a fresh or green man aboard the Friendship of Dundee, at the Davis Straits in 1824. [NRS.E508.130.8]

WALLACE, GEORGE, a sailor aboard the Friendship of Dundee, at the Davis Straits in 1824. [NRS.E508.130.8]

WALLACE, JAMES, tenant in Whinny Knowe of Oathlaw, testament, 1791, Comm. Brechin. [NRS]

WALLACE, PATRICK, a merchant in Brechin, a decreet, 1810. [NRS.CS36.1.29]

WALLACE, WILLIAM, an ale seller, was admitted as a burgess of Arbroath in 1797. [AA.18.941]

WANLESS, JOHN, a sailor of the Friendship of Dundee at the Davis Straits in 1824. [NRS.E508.130.8]

WANLESS, JOHN, surgeon aboard the Thomas in 1834. [HS.18.1.19] [McManus ms, Dundee]

WANN, WILLIAM, born 1788, a skipper in Cowgait, Dundee, 1818, [DD], master of the Fame in 1818, [DD], trading between Leith and Dundee in 1819, [NRS.E504.11.21]; died in 1829. [St Andrew's gravestone, Dundee]

WATSON, ALEXANDER, born 1737, a mariner in Dundee, died 1797, husband of Ann Adam, born 1749, died 1819. [Howff gravestone, Dundee]

WATSON, ANN, versus her husband Andrew Sward, a grocer in Dundee, a Process of Separation, 1809. [NRS.CC8.6.1373]

WATSON, Mrs ANN, in Inchbrayock Cottage, letters, 1829. [NRS.GD1.1678.33-37]

WATSON, DAVID, born 1715, a wright on Hawkhill, Dundee, died 1817, husband of Isabella Lowrence, born 1755, died 1818. [Howff gravestone, Dundee]

WATSON, DAVID, son of James Watson in Fearn, graduated MA from Marischal College, Aberdeen, in 1818, later schoolmaster in Cortachy. [MCA]

WATSON, DAVID, born 1737, a merchant in Murraygait, Dundee, died 1808. [Howff gravestone, Dundee]

WATSON, GEORGE, a sailor of the Friendship of Dundee at the Davis Straits in 1824. [NRS.E508.130.8]

WATSON, HENRY, son of Henry Watson a shipmaster in Dundee, a sailor in Downie Villa, California, by 1864. [NRS.S/H]

WATSON, Mrs ISABELLA, wife of Peter Watson a flax dresser in Dundee, died in Philadelphia, Pennsylvania, on 4 December 1861. [S.2033]

WATSON, JAMES, born 1750, stamp-master in Montrose, died 1831, husband of Margaret Morrison, born 1752, died 1839. [Montrose gravestone]

WATSON, JAMES, a baker in Wellgait, Dundee, in 1796. [DCA.B19.2.26/1]

WATSON, JAMES PYOT, a shipmaster in New York, nephew and heit of Margaret Ogilvie of Friock in 1812. [NRS.S/H]

WATSON, JAMES, born 1800, son of James Watson, [1778-1862], and his wife Elizabeth Mustard, [1806-1870], died in New Orleans, Louisiana, in 1839. [St Aidan's gravestone, Broughty Ferry]

WATSON, JOHN, born 1745, Rector of Dundee Grammar School, died 1809 in Glasgow, husband of Elisabeth Campbell, born 1745, died 1797. [Howff gravestone, Dundee]

WATSON, JOSEPH, a shipmaster, was admitted as a burgess of Arbroath in 1796. [AA.18.941]

WATSON, LILLIAS, daughter of John Watson of Thirty Acres, Arbroath, testament, 1797, Comm. St Andrews. [NRS]

WATSON, PETER, born 30 October 1816 in Arbroath, was educated at the University of Edinburgh, a linen manufacturer in Philadelphia, Pennsylvania, died there on 29 January 1890. [AP.352]

WATSON, RICHARD, was educated at St Andrews University, minister at Arbirlot from 1790 to 1829, husband of Isobel Balfour. [F.5.421]

WATSON, ROBERT, a shoemaker in Dundee, testament, 1796, Comm. Brechin. [NRS]

WATSON, ROBERT, fresh or green man aboard the Princess Charlotte of Dundee bound for the Davis Strait in 1824. [NRS.E508.129.8]

WATSON, WILLIAM, a divinity student, a burgess of Arbroath in 1790. [AA.18.941]

WATSON, WILLIAM, a carter, was admitted as a burgess of Arbroath in 1792. [AA.18.941]

WATT, ALEXANDER, a merchant in Dundee, and his wife Ann Marr, in Springfield, Dundee, parents of George Watt a merchant in Montreal, Canada, a deed, 1804. [NRS.RD3.336.34]

WATT, ARCHIBALD ANDERSON, son of James Watt a merchant in Dundee, a student at Marischal College, Aberdeen in 1840s, later in Australia. [MCA]

WATT, CHARLES, born 1753 in Montrose, a former soldier of Captain Campbell's Company of the 74$^{th}$ Regiment, settled in New Brunswick in the 1780s, died in Portland, New Brunswick, on 22 December 1841. [NBC.25.12.1841]

WATT, DANIEL, a shipbuilder in Montrose, testament, 1793, Comm. Brechin. [NRS]

WATT, GEORGE, a weaver, was admitted as a burgess of Arbroath in 1797. [AA.18.941]

WATT, ISAAC, a merchant burgess of Dundee, father of Alexander Watt a Major in the Service of the Honourable East India Company, was admitted as a burgess of Dundee on 4 January 1851. [DBR]

WATT, JAMES, a skipper in Tindall's Wynd, Dundee, in 1809, [DD], master of the William and Isabel of Dundee in 1798. [NRS.CE70.1.8]

WATT, JAMES, in Newton farm, St Vigeans, a victim of theft in 1824. [NRS.AD14.24.110]

WATT, JAMES, son of James Watt a merchant in Dundee, a student at Marischal College, Aberdeen in 1848, later in Australia. [MCA]

WATT, JOHN, of Denmiln, a merchant in Dundee, trading with Baltic ports between 1824 and 1829. [NRS.CS96.1329/2979]

WATT, JOHN, a cabinet-maker in Montrose, 1845. [NRS.CS280.7.70]

WATT, ROBERT, a brewer, was admitted as a burgess of Arbroath in 1792. [AA.18.941]

WATT, THOMAS, son of James Watt a merchant in Dundee, graduated MA from Marischal College, Aberdeen, in 1845. [MCA]

WATT, WILLIAM, a weaver, was admitted as a burgess of Arbroath in 1799. [AA.18.941]

WEBSTER, ALEXANDER, a manufacturer, was admitted as a burgess of Arbroath in 1797. [AA.18.941]

WEBSTER, ANDREW, a tenant in Newbigging of Balmuckie, later in Downieken, testament, 1792, Comm. Brechin. [NRS]

WEBSTER, FRANCIS, a merchant, was admitted as a burgess of Arbroath, 1792, [AA.18.941]

WEBSTER, GEORGE, son of James Webster a mariner in Dundee, a student at Marischal College in 1812. [MCA]

WEBSTER, GEORGE, son of Charles Webster in Forfar, died in Madras, India, on 30 June 1824. [AJ.4018]

WEBSTER, JAMES, a labourer in Arbroath, testament, 1800, Comm. St Andrews. [NRS]

WEBSTER, JAMES, a skipper in the Cowgait, Dundee, in 1782, and in the Seagait, Dundee, in 1818, [DD], master of the Ketty of Dundee in 1797, [NRS.CE70.1.8/77], of the Advice of Dundee in 1809, [DD], of the 144 ton brig Gowan in 1816, of the 190 ton brigantine Hector of Dundee in 1817-1818, trading between St Petersburg, Russia, and Dundee in 1818. [NRS.E504.11.21] [DPCA.740.768] [DD] [NRS.E504.11.20/21/22], and of the Erasmus of Dundee in 1824. [DSR]

WEBSTER, JOHN, tenant at Invereighty, later in Dundee, testament, 1800, Comm. Brechin. [NRS]

WEBSTER, JOHN, a baker in Kirriemuir, a cautioner in 1818. [NRS.CC8.8.145]

WEBSTER, JOHN, born 1827, a carter in Stobswell, Dundee, was accused of assault in 1847. [NRS.AD14.47.71]

WEBSTER, JOHN, an apprenticed, aboard the Dorothy of Dundee bound for the Davis Straits in 1825. [NRS.E508.130.8]

WEBSTER, LANCEMAN, a skipper in the Seagait, Dundee, 1818, 1825, master of the Hector of Dundee in 1824, and of the Advice in 1818, trading between St Petersburg, Russia, and Dundee in 1819; 1824, 1825. [DD][DSR] [NRS.E508; E504.24.21]

WEBSTER, ROBERT, harpooner of the Friendship of Dundee at the Davis Straits in 1824. [NRS.E508.130.8]

WEBSTER, ROBERT MACLAREN, son of John Webster in Kirriemuir, a student at Marischal College, Aberdeen, in 1840s. [MCA]

WEBSTER, ROBERT, born 1845, son of Francis Webster and his wife Janet Cooper, died in Sydney, New South Wales, Australia, on 23 July 1907. [Arbirlot gravestone]

WEBSTER, THOMAS, and his wife Margaret, parents of Arthur Webster, [1740-1819], a merchant in Montreal. [Howff gravestone, Dundee]

WEBSTER, THOMAS, hospital master of Dundee in 1793. [DCA.B19.3.26/1]

WEBSTER, THOMAS, born 1772, Captain of the 90$^{th}$ Regiment who fought in Egypt and the West Indies, died in Arbroath in 1845. [St Vigeans gravestone]

WEBSTER, THOMAS, son of James Webster a shipmaster in Montrose, died in Surinam on 23 August 1799, testament, 1803, Comm. Edinburgh. [NRS]

WEBSTER, WILLIAM, a slater in Dundee in 1798. [DCA.B19.3.27/2]

WEBSTER, WILLIAM, born 1825 in Angus, a civil engineer and land agent to the king, also Speaker in the House of Assembly, died in Honululu, the Sandwich Islands, [now Hawaii] on 23 March 1864. [AJ.6073]

WEBSTER, Captain, master of the Aylesford of Dundee, trading between St Petersburg, Russia, and Dundee in 1843. [MD.158]

WEDDERBURN, ALEXANDER, a heritor of Monifieth in 1806. [NRS.GD137.3592]

WEIR, DAVID, from Angus, graduated MA from King's College, Aberdeen, on 29 March 1811. [KCA]

WEIR, DAVID, a farmer at Warddykes, St Vigeans, a bond of caution, 1817. [NRS.CS271.684]

WEIR, JAMES, from Hallyburton in Angus, a florist in King's County, father of Jessie Weir who married Otto Heinigke, at Bay Ridge, Long Island, New York, in October 1874. [S.9773]

WELSH, ALEXANDER, born 1799, son of Andrew Welsh, a farmer, and his wife Ann Murray, at Lochlee, graduated MA from Marischal College in 1818, a surgeon who died under Lord Cochrane in 1822 during the Chilean War. [Lochlee gravestone][MCA]

WELSH, ANDREW, born 1740, farmer in Glen Effock, died 27 February 1814, husband of Ann Murray, born 1737, died 25 January 1825. [Lochlee gravestone]

WELSH, ANDREW, son of Andrew Welsh a farmer at Lochlee, a student at Marischal College, Aberdeen, in 1830s. [MCA]

WELSH, JAMES, in Kingston, Jamaica, was admitted as a burgess of Arbroath in 1789. [ABR]

WELSH, JOHN, born 1790, tenant in Glen Effock, died 7 December 1845, husband of Mary Falconer, born 1803, died 15 December 1859. [Lochlee gravestone]

WELSH, JOHN, master of the <u>Mercury of Dundee</u> trading between St Petersburg, Russia, and Dundee in 1818. [NRS.E504.11.21]

WELCH, ROBERT, a sailor aboard the <u>Dorothy of Dundee</u> bound for the Davis Straits in 1825. [NRS.E508.130.8]

WEMYSS, JOHN, a merchant in Dundee, testament, 1800, Comm. Brechin. [NRS]

WEMYSS, THOMAS, a merchant in Dundee in 1797. [NRS.CS97.172.88]

WEMYSS, WALTER, a merchant in Dundee in 1797. [NRS.CS97.172.88]

WEMYSS, WILLIAM, a greenman aboard the <u>Estridge of Dundee</u> from Dundee to Greenland on 25 March 1817, returned on 11 August 1817. [NRS.E508.129.8]

WESLEY, JOHN, master of the Ellangowan of Dundee in 1825, [DSR], and of the Confidence in 1828, [DPCA.1351] [NARA.mf237], testament, 1843. [NRS.SC45.31.6.6]

WESTERN, WALLACE, a Lieutenant of the 134th Regiment, was admitted as a burgess of Arbroath in 1795. [AA.18.941]

WHYTE, ALEXANDER. from Forfar, graduated MA from King's College, Aberdeen, on 30 March 1810. [KCA]

WHYTE, DAVID, from Angus, graduated MA from King's College, Aberdeen, in March 1818. [KCA]

WHITE, JAMES FARQUHAR, born 1820 in Letham, Angus, a merchant in New York before 1864, died in Balruddery near Dundee on 5 September 1884. [ANY]

WHITE, JOHN, a skipper on Yeaman Shore, Dundee, in 1818, [DD], master of the Fife Packet of Dundee in 1809, 1818, [DD], of the Defiance of Dundee and the Catherine of Dundee in 1825. [DSR]

WHITTET, JOHN, a corn merchant in Dundee, 1820-1821. [NRS.CS96.3528]

WIGHTON, JAMES, a manufacturer in Dundee, later in East Chapelshade of Dundee, testament, 1798, Comm. Brechin. [NRS]

WIGHTMAN or CARGILL, SUSAN, died in Arbroath on 16 November 1879, mother of Charles Cargill an engineer in Australia. [NRS.S/H]

WIGHTON, JAMES, born 1767, died 1843, and his wife Jean Watson, born 1768, died 1815, parents of George Wighton an engineer in New Orleans, Louisiana. [Old Mains gravestone, Dundee]

WIGHTON, JAMES, born 1828, son of William Wighton and his wife Mary Taws, died in Castlemain, Australia, on 10 September 1860. [Eastern gravestone, Dundee]

WIGHTON, MARTHIEW, widow of .... Wallace, in Dundee, testament, 1800, Comm. Brechin. [NRS]

WIGTOWN, WILLIAM, from Stonyruives, Liff and Benvie, a factory worker in Montrose, was accused of forgery in 1820. [NRS.AD14.20.137]

WILKIE, GEORGE, a merchant in Dundee, 1791, 1798. [DCA.B19.3.27/262][NRS.SC20.33.13]

WILKIE, JAMES, son of George Wilkie a merchant in Dundee, a student at Marischal College, Aberdeen, in 1811. [MCA]

WILKIE, JAMES, born 1799, third son of George Wilkie of Auchlishie, a merchant in New Orleans, Louisiana, died on 18 August 1834. [Dundee gravestone]

WILKIE, ROBERT, born 1725, a merchant shipmaster in Arbroath, died 1799, husband of Christian Petrie, a sasine. [NRS.RS34.22.178] [Arbroath Abbey gravestone]

WILKIE, ROBERT, born 1734, a wright in Dundee, a sasine in 1770, died 1827, husband of [1] Elisabeth Fyfe, born 1739, died 1787, [2] Elizabeth Herald, born 1767, died 1826. [Howff gravestone, Dundee]; [NRS.RS35.67]

WILL, ANDREW, clerk to the Town Clerk of Dundee in 1798. [DCA.B19.3.27/6]

WILL, CHARLES, born 1782, a mason in Dryenook, Lochlee, died 14 October 1854. [Lochlee gravestone]

WILL, ISABELLA, a dressmaker, was granted a tack in Edzell, in 1843. [NRS.GD45.16.1932]

WILL, WILLIAM, gardener in Craigie, testament, 1797, Comm. Brechin. [NRS]

WILLIAMS, SARAH, born 1726, widow of Samuel Williams the President of Grenada, died in Dundee on 14 September 1809. [SM.71.799]

WILLIAMSON, JAMES, a shipmaster in Montrose, testament, 1800, Comm. Brechin. [NRS]

WILLIAMSON, JOHN, a weaver, was admitted as a burgess of Arbroath in 1795. [AA.18.941]

WILLIAMSON, PETER, born 1741, died 1810. [Howff gravestone, Dundee]

WILLOCKS, ......, in Muirside of Craig, parish of Logie Pert, was the victim of assault in 1832. [NRS.AD14.32.21]

WILSON, DAVID, a weaver, was admitted as a burgess of Arbroath in 1797. [AA.18.941]

WILSON, DAVID H., from Brechin, graduated MA from King's College, Aberdeen, in March 1849, later minister at Renton. [KCA]

WILSON, EDWARD, an upholsterer in Dundee, father of David Wilkie Wilson who died in Adelaide, Australia, on 29 April 1881. [Western gravestone, Dundee]

WILSON, GEORGE ROBERTSON, born 1829, son of John Wilson and his wife Isabella Hood, died in Ballarat, Australia, on 16 June 1880. [Constitution Road gravestone, Dundee]

WILSON, JAMES, jr., born 1780 in Angus, a merchant who was naturalised in Charleston, South Carolina, on 10 December 1805. [NARA.M1183.1]

WILSON, JOHN, a lease in Linlathen in 1844. [NRS.GD16.28.550]; born 1805, died 1869, husband of Margaret Hood, born 1815, died 1908, parents of Thomas H. Wilson in Eaton, Colorado. [Lintrathen gravestone]

WILSON, JOHN, a cabinetmaker in Dundee, and his wife Margaret Miller, parents of David Wilson a blacksmith, and of John Wilson a tenter, both in Boston, Massachusetts, by 1871. [NRS.SH.1871]

WILSON, WILLIAM, sailor aboard the <u>Estridge of Dundee</u> bound for the Davis Straits in 1824. [NRS.E508.129.8]

WINDRUM, JAMES, a weaver, was admitted as a burgess of Arbroath in 1797. [AA.18.941]

WISHART, JEAN, in Dundee, testament, 1798, Comm. Brechin. [NRS]

WISHART, JOHN, a skipper in Tindall's Wynd, Dundee, in 1809, and in Peter Street, Dundee, in 1825, [DD], master of the London Packet of Dundee, in 1809, 1824, of the Union of Dundee in 1818, and of the British King of Dundee in 1825, [DD][DRS], testament, 1845. [NRS.SC45.31.7.222]

WISHART, MARGARET, born 1782, of High Street, Arbroath, was jointly accused of the murder by poison of Jean Wishart there in 1827. [NRS.AD14.27.179]

WOOD, JAMES, a manufacturer in Brechin, versus Robert Forrester, a decreet 1816. [NRS.CS14.188.15]

WOOD, JAMES, a merchant in Lundie Mill, 18... [NRS.CS233.SEQN.W1.35]

WOOD, JOHN, son of John Wood a tailor in Careston, a student at Marischal College, Aberdeen, 1811-1815. [MCA]

WOOD, MARTIN BRYDEN, born 1837 in Broughty Ferry, son of Reverend John Wood and his wife Annabella Bryden, died in Sydney, Australia, on 15 April 1918. [F.5.312]

WRIGHT, FRANCES, born 6 September 1785 in 136 Nethergait, Dundee, daughter of James Wright a merchant, emigrated to America via Liverpool, was naturalised in New York on 16 November 1818, founded the Nashuba Commune in Tennessee, died 13 December 1852; a deed 1819, [NRS.RD5.228.341]

WRIGHT, JAMES, the younger, a merchant in Dundee in 1791. [DCA.B19.3.27/262]

WRIGHT, JAMES, a weaver, was admitted as a burgess of Arbroath, 1797. [AA.18.941]

WRONGHAM, WILLIAM, born 1756, a skipper in 32 Murraygait, Dundee, 1809, 1818, [DD], a burgess of Dundee in 1797, [DBR], master of the John of Dundee in 1796, of the Eliza of Dundee in 1797, [NRS.CE70.1.8/52, 70], of the Eliza of Dundee in 1818, and of the Antelope of Dundee in 1824, [DSR][NRS.E504.11.20]; died in 1835. [Howff gravestone, Dundee], testament, 1835. [NRS.SC45.31.2.572]

WYLLIE, DAVID, born 1773, a merchant, died in Montrose on 10 December 1825. [SM.97.128]

WYLLIE, JAMES, born 2 January 1795, son of William Wyllie and his wife Annie Stupart, died in Russia on 21 October 1850. [Howff gravestone, Dundee]

WYLLIE, or AITKEN, JAMES, son of James Wyllie a merchant in Kirriemuir, a student at Marischal College, Aberdeen, in 1820s, graduated LL.D. in 1855. [MCA]

WYSE, ISABEL, born 1713, died 1803, widow od David Low late in the Mains of Barras. [Montrose Episcopal gravestone]

YEAMAN, JAMES, born 15 September 1845 in Oathlaw, son of Robert Yeaman and his wife Susan Scott, 'sometime in California', died in Dundee on 1 December 1906. [Oathlaw gravestone]

YEAMAN, JOHN, in Union Bank, Kirriemuir, a victim of forgery in 1832. [NRS.AD14.32.27]

YEAMAN, WILLIAM, of Balbeuchly, a merchant in Dundee, son of George Yeaman a merchant and Provost of Dundee, in 1799. [NRS.SC20.36.15] [DCA.B18.3.27/253] merchant and Provost of Dundee, in 1799. [NRS.SC20.36.15] [DCA.B18.3.27/253]

YOUNG, ANDREW, master of the Annie of Arbroath trading between Montrose and Inverness in 1811. [NRS.E504.17.8]

YOUNG, ANDREW, a labourer at the North Port of Brechin, was accused of mobbing and rioting in the High Street of Brechin in 1830. [NRS.AD14.30.89]

YOUNG, DAVID, born 1744, a merchant in Montrose, died 1814, husband of Jean Smith, born 1753, died 1827. [Montrose gravestone]

YOUNG, DAVID, steersman aboard the Dorothy of Dundee bound for the Davis Straits in 1825. [NRS.E508.130.8]

YOUNG, GEORGE, born 1789 in Cortachy, a merchant who emigrated via London to America, settled in Alabama, was naturalised in New York on 10 November 1817. [Court of Common Pleas Records, NY]

YOUNG, GEORGE, was imprisoned for assaulting a Revenue Officer in Cortachy-Clova in 1824. [NRS.JC26.1824.82]

YOUNG, JAMES, a tailor in Redford, Carmyllie, testament, 15 March 1793, Comm. Brechin. [NRS]

YOUNG, JAMES, a shipmaster in Dundee, testament, 11 April 1798, Comm. Brechin. [NRS]

YOUNG, Dr JAMES, formerly in Antigua later in Montrose in 1809 [reference in NRS.RD4.293.503]

YOUNG, JAMES, born 1800 in Dundee, son of George Young, a weaver, and his wife Mary, was educated at the University of St Andrews, was a minister in British Guiana from 1841 to 1844, died in Broughty Ferry on 3 November 1882. [F.7.676]

YOUNG, JOHN, master of the Neptune of Dundee trading between St Petersburg, Russia, and Dundee in 1818. [NRS.E504.11.21]

YOUNG, JOHN, born 1814, a porter in Dundee, died in Sydney, Australia, on 20 August 1861, [St Peter's gravestone, Dundee]

YOUNG, JOHN, and Andrew Young, were accused of sheep stealing in Brechin in 1831. [NRS.JC26.1831.36]

YOUNG, NATHANIEL, master of the Two Brothers of Dundee in 1809. [DD]

YOUNG, ROBERT, master of the Mentor of Dundee in 1809. [DD]

YOUNG, ROBERT, born 1844, son of James Young and his wife Margaret Martin, died in Tacoma, USA, on 31 January 1889. [Rosehill gravestone, Montrose]

YOUNG, SAMUEL, a fresh or green man aboard the Estridge of Dundee bound for the Davis Straits in 1824. [NRS.E508.129.8]

YOUNG, THOMAS, master of the Betsey of Dundee in 1809. [DD]

YOUNG, WILLIAM, a skipper in Tindall's Wynd, Dundee, in 1809, and in Castle Court, Dundee, in 1818, [DD], master of the <u>Favourite of Dundee</u> in 1809, [DD]

YOUNG, WILLIAM, line manager aboard the <u>Dorothy of Dundee</u> bound for the Davis Straits in 1825. [NRS.E508.130.8]

YOUNG, WILLIAM, born 1828, son of William Young and his wife Isabella Tutin, died in St Ann's, Barbados, on 19 December 1848. [Howff gravestone, Dundee]

YOUNG, WILLIAM, born 1829, son of William Young and his wife Marjory Turnbull, died in New South Wales, Australia, in 1861. [St Aidan's gravestone, Broughty Ferry]

YOUNG, WILLIAM, from Kirriemuir, graduated MA from King's College, Aberdeen, in March 1851, later a United Presbyterian minister in Selkirk and Glasgow. [KCA]

YOUNG, Captain, master of the <u>Emma of Dundee</u> from Dundee via Aberdeen bound for Sydney, Cape Breton, Canada, in 1848. [AJ]

YULE, ADAM, master of the <u>Australia of Dundee</u> from Dundee with passengers bound for Australia in 1840. [W.I.81/85]

YULE, ELIZABETH, in Mains of Craigo, Logie, 1809. [NRS.GD1.196.9]

www.ingramcontent.com/pod-product-compliance
Lightning Source LLC
Chambersburg PA
CBHW052100230426
43662CB00036B/1707